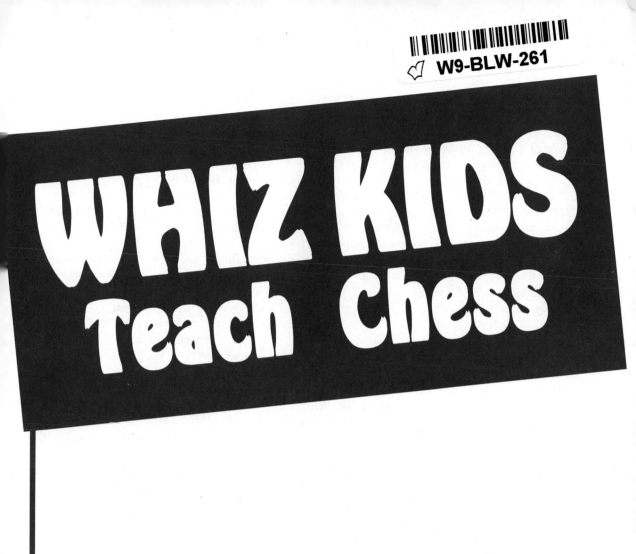

ABOUT THE AUTHOR

Eric Schiller, widely considered one of the world's foremost chess analysts, writers, and teachers, is internationally recognized for his definitive works on openings. He is the author of 87 chess books including Cardoza Publishing's definitive series on openings, *World Champion Openings, Standard Chess Openings*, and *Unorthodox Chess Openings* — an exhaustive opening library of more than 1700 pages. He's also the author of *Encyclopedia of Chess Wisdom, Gambit Opening Repertoire for White, Gambit Opening Repertoire for Black, Complete Defense to King Pawn Openings, Complete Defense to Queen Pawn Openings*, and multiple other chess titles for Cardoza Publishing. (For listings of all chess titles published by Cardoza Publishing, go online to www.cardozapub.com.)

Eric Schiller is a National and Life Master, an International Arbiter of F.I.D.E., and the official trainer for many of America's top young players. He has recently been reappointed as official coach of America's best players under 18 to represent the United States at the Chess World Championships. He has also presided over world championship matches dating back to 1983, runs prestigious international tournaments, and has been interviewed dozens of times in major media throughout the world. His games have been featured in leading chess journals and newspapers including the venerable New York Times. Schiller has helped design some of the most popular chess software being used today. Eric Schiller's web site is www.chessworks.com.

Eric, who has trained many of the Whiz Kids and other chess prodigies, adds the experiences of four decades at the chessboard to bring readers of this book the whole world of chess.

Eric is the senior editor of the free online chess magazine, www.chesscity.com

---

NEW CARDOZA PUBLISHING BOOKS BY ERIC SCHILLER

STANDARD CHESS OPENINGS - The new standard on opening chess play, references every important opening and variation played - more than 3,000 opening strategies! The standard reference book necessary for competitive play. *A must have!!!* 768 pgs, $24.95.

UNORTHODOX CHESS OPENINGS - The comprehensive guide to contains more than 1,200 weird, contentious, controversial, unconventional, arrogant and outright strange opening strategies. Great against unprepared opponents. *Great Fun!* 528 pgs, $24.95.

WORLD CHAMPION OPENINGS - Covers the essential opening theory and moves of every major chess opening and variation as played by *all* the world champions. Learn the insights, concepts and secrets as used by the greatest players of all time. 384 pages, $18.95

COMPLETE DEFENSE TO QUEEN PAWN OPENINGS - This aggressive counterattacking repertoire covers Black opening systems against virtually all chess opening except for 1.e4 (including flank games), based on the powerful Tarrasch Defense. 288 pages, $16.95.

COMPLETE DEFENSE TO KING PAWN OPENINGS - Learn a complete defensive system against 1.e4 based on the mighty Caro-Kann, a favorite weapon of many great players. All White's options are shown with plans for Black to combat them all. 288 pages, $16.95.

WHIZ KIDS TEACH CHESS *Eric Schiller and the Whiz Kids* - Today's greatest young stars, from 10 to 17 years of age–tells of their successes, failures, world travels, and love of the game. At the heart of this book is a chess primer with large diagrams, clear explanations, and winning ideas. Lots of photos, 144 large format pages, $14.95.

ENCYCLOPEDIA OF CHESS WISDOM, *The Essential Concepts and Strategies of Smart Chess Play by Eric Schiller* The most important concepts, strategies, tactics, wisdom, and thinking that every chessplayer must know, plus the gold nuggets of knowledge behind every attack and defense, all in one volume. 432 pages, $19.95.

Get online now to learn more about upcoming titles! www.cardozapub.com

---

WHIZ KIDS
Teach Chess

Eric Schiller
& the Whiz Kids

Vinay Bhat
Jennie Frenklakh
Matthew Ho
Gabe Kahane
Irina Krush
Jordy Mont-Reynaud
Asuka Nakamura
Hikaru Nakamura
Greg Shahade
Jennifer Shahade

Cardoza Publishing

CARDOZA PUBLISHING

Authoritative and Readable Books for Chess Players
- Chess is Our Game -

This book is dedicated to all of my present and former students. I hope chess continues to be fun and a refuge from a busy life.

Special thanks to Peter Kurzdorfer, whose previous work with me is the basis for the teaching materials here. Thanks to all of the young players who contributed to this book: Vinay Bhat, Jennie Frenklakh, Gabe Kahane, Irina Kush, Jordy Mont-Reynaud, Matthew Ho, Asuka and Hikaru Nakamura, and Jennifer and Greg Shahade. All of their parents, too!

Photographs come courtesy of Elizabeth Karnazes (front cover, back cover Irina-Gabe game, and pages 8, 28, 37, 47, 51, 52, 57-Greg, 60, 62, 76, 118), Pamela Olson (pages 23, 91, back cover), Mont-Reynoud family (page 117), Ho family (page 32), others courtesy of Eric Schiller. Pictured in the front photo, starting from left front and going clockwise around the table: Gabe, Irina, Hikaru, Asuka, Jennifer, Jennie, Vinay, Matthew, Zachary (who, with brother Alex, is working his way toward Whiz Kid status), Jordy. Photo shot in Kona, Hawaii, at the Cardoza US Open.

Special mention must be made of Avery Cardoza, our publisher, whose generous sponsorship of the US Open gave all of the young masters valuable experience on and off the board in Hawaii! Saitek Industries' sponsorship of the US Masters made the experience doubly exciting. Many of the games in this book were played in these sponsored events, and would not exist otherwise.

Finally, thanks to all those who provided background information for the book, including Tom Dorsch, Ron Henley, Paul Hodges, Peter Kurzdorfer, and others at the United States Chess Federation.

First Edition

Library of Congress Catalog Card No: 98-71032
ISBN: 1-58042-007-9

CARDOZA PUBLISHING

PO Box 1500 Cooper Station, New York, NY 10276
Phone (718)743-5229 • Fax(718)743-8284 •
Email:cardozapub@aol.com
Web Site - www.cardozapub.com

Write for your free catalogue of gaming and chess books,
equipment, software, and computer games.

TABLE OF CONTENTS

HOW TO USE THIS BOOK

If you are not familiar with the game of chess, then you should start by reading the chapter on the rules of the game. If you already know how to play chess, but don't know how to follow a chess game, read the section on chess notation. Then you can enjoy the chess games and positions in the book. More advanced players can dive right in to the discussion, but may wish to learn about the chess titles and rating system to understand the accomplishments of the young players. A chapter is dedicated to that topic.

Teachers can use the materials in this book as part of a complete chess course, starting with beginners but useful even for experienced players.

Everyone can follow the careers of the prodigies on the Internet. If you want to get involved with tournament chess, there is a chapter on chess resources, online and traditional, to help you along.

INTRODUCTION

We will take you on an exciting journey to the world of chess in this book. Through the eyes of the *Whiz Kids*, ten young prodigies who will act as our guides, you'll not only see what the world of chess has offered our young stars and can offer you, but you'll get insights and practical information on how to become a better player. The Whiz Kids will share the excitement of playing chess in Europe, Hawaii, and other exotic destinations around the world, the thrill of beating Grandmasters, and will talk about and show us their greatest triumphs and failures.

You don't need to know anything about chess to follow their exploits, but for new players and beginners, a complete chess course is included, showing you how to write and read chess notation, how to make all the moves so that you can start playing immediately, and how to use strategies to improve your game, so that you can enjoy the artistic accomplishments of our young stars. You'll also find out how to play anywhere in the world through a chess organization or via the Internet.

But there is much more here. We present the best games of each young star, their worst mistake, and some tales of joy, wonder, and horror on and off the chessboard. You'll meet FIDE Master Vinay Bhat, the 14-year old Pan American Champion and World Youth Championship Bronze Medallist. Woman FIDE Master Irina Krush is the same age, and holds the Pan American Girls Title. She's already played in the invitational U.S. Women's Championship, as have contributors Jennie Frenklakh and National Master Jennifer Shahade, both 17, who have all represented the United States at the World Youth Championships.

So has National Master Jordy Mont-Reynaud, 14, who smashed Bobby Fischer's record to become the youngest National Master in America. He held that record only briefly, because Vinay beat it, but in turn lost it to Hikaru Nakamura, America's youngest National Master ever. At the age of 10, he is already a veteran of international competition, and his older brother Asuka has seen his own records fall! Matthew Ho is the latest prodigy, and he'll be representing the United States at the World Under-10 Championship in Spain this year. Candidate Master Gabe Kahane, 17, won the Calchess Scholastic Blitz title ahead of several of our other young stars, and tied for third at the 1997 National High School Championship.

As you'll see, the life of a chess prodigy involves a lot of hard work, but the rewards are more than worth the effort, by far! Chess tournaments, especially those which involve a week or more at a nice resort, can be a lot of fun.

Okay, let's play chess!

THE GAME OF CHESS!

Chess is a great game, with a history of entertaining and challenging players that date back over a thousand years, possibly even two thousand years! It is not difficult to learn to play, but requires concentration and practice to play well. Tens of thousands of books have been written on chess, but its mysteries still defy solution by mortal or computer brains.

Chess is a contest where two players take turns moving pieces on a board, trying to trap the most important piece, the king. There are different types of pieces, and each has its own set of rules. There is no element of luck in chess; a game can only be lost as a result of an error by one of the players. The game is so rich that there are opportunities to find a winning plan in most games.

Currently, 157 nations hold membership in the world chess organization, and the game is known to be played in many of the remaining countries. In fact, chess is the second most popular sport in the world behind soccer. You might think that chess does not qualify as a sport because it is not an *athletic* sport, however, the stars of the game must be in top physical condition for the grueling tournament pace of six to seven hours per day, often for almost two weeks with only a single rest day. Mind sports do not allow the neglect of the body!

The International Olympic Committee recognizes chess as administered by the World Chess Federation. They realize the need to have some Olympic sports which do not require the luck of being born with a healthy and exceptionally gifted body. Everyone can play chess despite physical disabilities. Competitive chess is played by many people who cannot even see the board!

When IBM put their most powerful machines to work serving up information on the first match between World Champion Garry Kasparov and their Deep Blue computer, the interest on the internet brought it crashing down. No one had anticipated the millions of hits it would generate.

There is big money involved for the professional players. The prize fund for the World Champion is $3,000,000! Many tournaments have prize funds in excess of $100,000, and even short matches can bring a nice paycheck of $50,000 and more. Major open tournaments such as the National Open in Las Vegas draw over a thousand players. The best players have all of their expenses covered, and often get an "appearance" fee of $10,000 or more just for showing up! Not bad.

Chess is a young person's game. The average age of professional chessplayers has been dropping steadily. The first World Champion Wilhelm Steinitz was 58 years, 10 days when he lost his title on May 26, 1894. The current World Champion, Garry Kasparov is the youngest. He won the title on Nov 9, 1985 at age 22 years, 210 days.

You might expect that powerful brains and computers would have figured out everything there is to know about the game, but in fact a "solution" for chess is not even being approached. Yes, a computer did defeat the World Champion in a short exhibition match, but the computer chickened out when challenged to a match under serious match conditions. Still, the search to create the perfect chess-playing machine continues. The task brings together a collection of specialists in mathematics, computer science, artificial intelligence, and others.

Just as we admire artistry in athletic sports, beauty in chess has always been highly regarded. It is difficult to describe chess beauty. Sometimes we admire a game for its bold sacrifices, other times for a fine strategy. In many cases, we are struck by a surprising move or piece formation.

Thus, it is not surprising that chess if often found in art. Indeed, many of the great artists and intellectuals have relaxed (or not!) with a game of chess for centuries. Entire books have been written on the subject of chess and the arts, so here is just a sample of books, films, television and musical connections to the Royal Game.

BOOKS

Many famous writers have a long had strong connection with the game of chess. As a matter of fact, William Caxton's *The Play of the Chesse* was one of the very first books printed in English, back in the 15th century! William Golding, author of *Lord of the Flies,* actually lost a correspondence game because the news of his Nobel Prize reached him just at a critical moment in the game.

We have all read or seen Lewis Carroll's, *Through the Looking Glass*, which has a hilarious chess game. Chess was a direct subject of famous books by Vladimir Nabokov (*The Defense*) and Walter Tevis (*The Queen's Gambit*). Short stories include Jorge Luis Borges' *Chess*, Poul Anderson's *The Immortal Game*. The great American master, O. Henry, loved to compete at the chessboard, and famous writers such as Samuel Beckett use chess frequently. His play *Murphy* contains an annotated chess game! Even old Shakespeare mentions the game a few times, and there is a painting showing him playing. The great Russian poet Alexander Pushkin was almost obsessed by chess.

When writers gather, a chess set is often put to use! For an excellent survey of chess in literature, check out Burt Hochberg's, *The 64-Square Looking Glass*. If you read a lot, you'll find chess mentioned all the time.

FILMS

No one has compiled a complete listing of films and actors, but it would be the size of a phone book, perhaps. Chess is ideally suited to the film industry, where often people have to wait around between scenes.

Chess is found throughout such classics as Begman's *Seventh Seal*, and modern films like *Searching for Bobby Fischer*. Famous chess scenes include Faye Dunaway and Steve McQueen in *The Thomas Crown Affair*. The chess scene in the beginning of *From Russia with Love* is taken from a real game played by World Champion Boris Spassky. The film version of Ilf and Petrov's *The Twelve Chairs*, with a comic chess scene, was directed by Mel Brooks, who also slipped chess into his more famous *Blazing Saddles*. Chess won't seem to die out in the future, to judge by such films as Ridley Scott's *Blade Runner*.

Humphrey Bogart plays chess in *Casablanca*, but didn't need a stunt double for the scene — he played chess all the time, even for money at a chess café. A number of Bogarts games have been published. John Wayne played frequently, but was hardly in Bogie's class. Marlon Brando also amused himself during breaks by playing chess. Actresses such as Katherine Hepburn and Zsa Zsa Gabor are among the famous stars who played chess. Many directors, including Ingmar Bergman, Stanley Kubrick (*2001* has a famous scene with a human vs. computer) and Woody Allen play chess avidly. This is not surprising, since manipulating people is what they do for a living!

TELEVISION

Television moves at a faster pace, so there isn't as much time to play on the set. Chess has played a significant and more direct role in many television shows. It is a recurring theme in the classic show *The Prisoner*, and is featured in many episodes of *Dr. Who*, taking center stage in the conclusion of the episode *The Curse of Fenric*, where the game is revealed as a linking factor in many previous stories. Chess pops up in many sitcoms, probably because stars such as Alan Alda (*M.A.S.H*), Bill Cosby (many shows), Patrick McGoohan (*The Prisoner*) and Stephen Fry (*Jeeves*) are fanatical players. Chess even turns up in a lot of commercials!

If you are spending too much time in front of a TV set, consider playing chess instead. At least you don't have to deal with the ads!

MUSIC

So many performers and composers have taken chess seriously that it might be easier to list those who never played at all! From Prokofiev to Frank Sinatra to Phish, even Johnny (Rudolf the red-nosed reindeer) Marks, chessboards travel with all sorts of musicians. There was even a hit musical about chess, called, inventively, *Chess*, as well as a ballet (Arthur Bliss wrote *Checkmate*). Chess is a favorite pastime of musicians everywhere.

CHESS NOTATION

Chessplayers like to record their games, and we have records of games from a thousand years ago! You never know when you will come up with a brilliant game that will be published all over the world, so it is best to keep a record of all of them, even the ones you lose, because those often contain valuable lessons. Almost all tournaments require you to write down the moves, so you may as well learn right away. If you are unfamiliar with the code used for reading and writing about chess, this section will explain it all and help you follow the games we present in this book.

Recording a game score isn't very hard at all, once you know how. The board is divided into a grid, with letters from a to h along the base and numbers from 1 to 8 along the side, so that files are lettered and ranks are numbered. Each square thus has a name, consisting of a letter and a number.

At the beginning of the game the pieces are in their original positions.

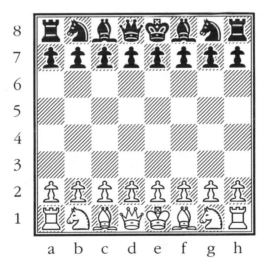

We refer to the horizontal rows as **ranks** and the vertical columns as **files**. The ranks are numbered 1-8, from White's point of view. The files are designated by letters, from a-h. After you get used to playing out chess games from the notation, you won't need any help in remembering them. For this introduction, however, we'll add the letters and numbers to help you follow the discussion.

In order to keep track of a game, you'll need a scoresheet. On it, there are spaces for White and Black moves, and they are all numbered. You start by filling out the names of the players and the date. A White move and a Black move make up one move. White moves are written on the left hand side and Black moves are written on the right hand side.

THE MOVES

Each move on the board can be described with six pieces of information:

1. The name of the piece being moved.
2. The square the piece is moving from.
3. The square the piece is moving to.
4. Whether or not the move captures an enemy piece.
5. Whether or not the enemy king is placed in check.
6. The place in the game where the move was played.

The most common form of notation is the *American style*. We start by indicating the number of the move. We use a number followed by a period. Then we add an abbreviation for the piece being moved.

The pieces have the following abbreviations: king is **K**; queen is **Q**; rook is **R**; bishop is **B**; knight is **N** (not K, because that is reserved for the king). The pawn has no abbreviation. Don't ask why it's not "P." It may be to make the notation more "efficient," though in reality it just makes it more complicated! The lowly pawn gets left out, but as long as there is no other capital letter indicated, then we understand that it must be a pawn move.

After the abbreviation for the piece, the square the piece lands on is usually indicated next. However, we can give some information about the square that the piece is moving from, but only if we have to. We will skip this for the moment, but return to it soon.

We'll make our first move, with the king pawn moving two squares forward. We write, **1.e4.** The position after the move is shown in the diagram:

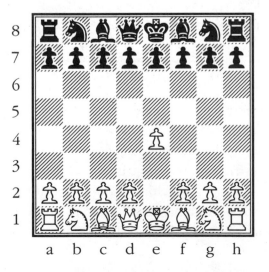

Now the pawn rests on the 4th square of the e-file. If you need to, count the letters from the left edge of the diagram (a, b, c, d, e) and count up from the bottom (1, 2, 3, 4). It will take a little time for you to master the chessboard in your mind, but you will find that it comes easily enough over time.

Now suppose we want to describe Black's reply, also moving the pawn on the kingside to a position two squares in front of the king.

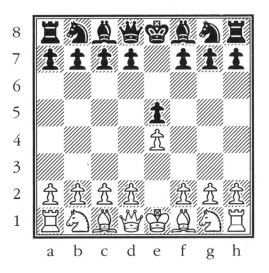

This move would be written **1...e5**. We use an ellipsis (...) to indicate that it is not White's move, but Black's. If we want to describe the entire game so far, we write simply **1.e4 e5**. In this instance, we didn't use the ellipsis, since the White and Black moves are represented together. As you can see, the White move is always shown first, then the Black move after.

Now let's say that White brings the bishop to b5.

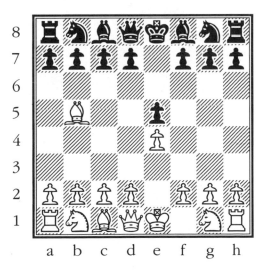

SAMPLE CHESS SCORESHEET

	Time control: 40 moves in 120 minutes.	Round 1 2 3 4 5 6 7 8 9 Board	Result White won Draw Black won	CARDOZA PUBLISHING
White:			Mark here if game should be considered for publication or best game prize:	
Black:				

#	White	Black	#		
1	e4	e5	21		
2	Bb5	Nc6	22		
3	Nf3	a6	23		
4	Bxc6		24		
5			25		
6			26		
7			27		
8			28		
9			29		
10			30		
11			31		
12			32		
13			33		
14			34		
15			35		
16			36		
17			37		
18			38		
19			39		
20			40		

This event is held under the auspices and rules of the United States Chess Federation. Each player is required to turn in the top copy of this scoresheet at the end of the game. Both players should sign each scoresheet below.

That move is written **2.Bb5**. The "2" indicates White's second move, the Bb5 shows that a bishop has moved to the b5 square. The game now reads **1.e4 e5; 2.Bb5.**

Black responds by bringing a knight to c6. We notate that as **2...Nc6**. We don't have to say which knight, because only one of the Black knights can move to c6. Let's try a few more moves. We'll let the game continue with White bringing a knight to f3, transposing, by the way, into the Spanish Game.

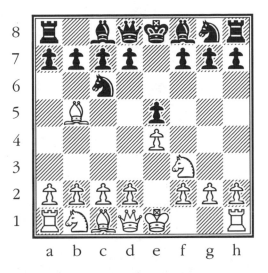

That's **3.Nf3**, giving us **1.e4 e5; 2.Bb5 Nc6; 3.Nf3**. Black responds by moving the a-pawn forward one square, attacking the White bishop. **3...a6.**

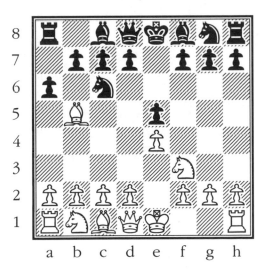

Now let us introduce a new element. We will capture the knight with our bishop. Because we are capturing an enemy piece, we add an "x" between the piece and a capture.

We represent the move with **4.Bxc6**. Annotation of the game so far would be as follows: **1.e4 e5; 2.Bb5 Nc6; 3.Nf3 a6; 4.Bxc6**.

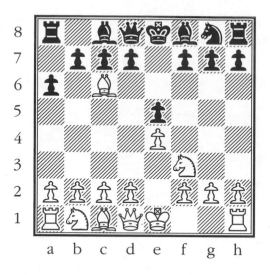

Earlier we said that we'll only mention the square the piece is leaving from if we have to. Now we have to. We can't just write 4...xc6 because that would not tell us which of the two possible pawn captures are possible.

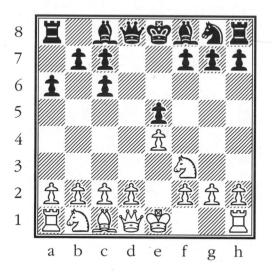

Because we need to clarify the situation, we add the file that the pawn is leaving from: **4...dxc6**. We see that it is the pawn on the *d-file* that is making the capture, not the pawn on the b-file.

Now it is White's turn, and let's suppose that the sensible move of castling takes place.

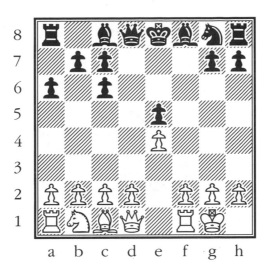

Our system has no easy way of combining the king and rook moves, so instead there is a simple convention. We use two zeros separated by a hyphen to indicate castling on the kingside (castling short): **5.0-0**. For queenside castling, we would add another hyphen and another zero "0-0-0".

Our game so far is **1.e4 e5; 2.Bb5 Nc6; 3.Nf3 a6; 4.Bxc6 dxc6; 5.0-0**. Let's try a few more moves, without commentary. **5...f6; 6.Nxe5 fxe5**. These moves should be easy to spot. We have now reached the following position:

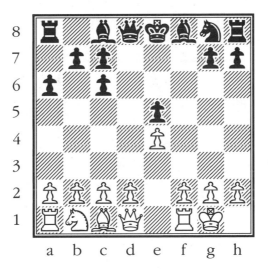

I have chosen these moves just to illustrate the last important part of the notation. If White now plays the queen to h5, the enemy king will be in check. We indicate this by appending a suffix in the form of a plus "+" sign. We are at move seven, so the notation is **7.Qh5+**. Our entire game can be described as **1.e4 e5; 2.Bb5 Nc6; 3.Nf3 a6; 4.Bxc6 dxc6; 5.0-0 f6; 6.Nxe5 fxe5;. 7.Qh5+**.

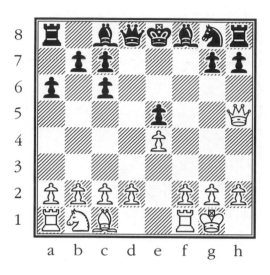

An actual checkmate will be indicated by "++" or "#".

One final point. If you are lucky enough to promote a pawn into a queen, it is written by marking the square that the pawn promotes onto, affixing an equal "=" sign, and then indicating the piece the pawn is promoted to. For example, e8=Q means that the pawn moves to the e8 square and is replaced by a queen.

THE SYMBOLS

There are many special symbols used in specialist chess literature, but in this book, words are generally used instead for easier comprehension. Still, we use a few symbols to point out moves of special, or doubtful, merit.

> ! = a good move
> ? = a bad move
> !? = an interesting move
> ?!= a dubious move
> !!= a brilliant move
> ??= a terrible move

These symbols are not to be used while playing the game. You add them later when studying, or, if you are playing against a human opponent, during the "post-mortem" which is what we call post-game analysis.

MEET THE STARS

Let's meet the young stars who will be accompanying us on our journey through the world of chess. They come from all over the United States, and range in age from 10 to 19. We'll look briefly at their careers to date and some of the things they like to do when not playing chess.

All of these players have competed in national and international competitions. Most have participated in the Pan American or World Youth Championships, two of the most prestigious tournaments for young chessplayers. You might find it strange to compare their ages at the time with the official age classifications but the trick is that it is the age of the player on January 1 that usually determines eligibility.

The World Youth Championship is held every year. There are competitions for every even-numbered age group from 10 to 18. All players who have not reached the age of 10 on January 1 of the year of the competition are eligible for the Under-10. There are 5 age groups at the World Youth, and there is also a World Junior Championship for those under 20. Each competition has a boys section and a girls section. Each country can send one representative, not counting players who qualify from special events such as the Pan American Championship.

The Pan American Championship is second in importance only to the World Youth Championship. Only players from North, South, and Central America can compete. Winners of each section earn the title of FIDE Master from the World Chess Federation (FIDE).

The United States holds a bewildering variety of scholastic events. The most important are the US Junior (Under-21) and US Cadet (Under-16). There are also National High School, Junior High School and Elementary Championships, and a separate National Grade School Championship which awards titles for each school grade from kindergarten through 12th grade.

Each state also holds scholastic championships, but often the best players miss these because they conflict with other important national and international events. The biggest incentive to playing is a potential invitation to the Denker Tournament of High School Champions, held in conjunction with the US Open each year. In some states, such as New York and California, our young stars must compete against each other for the one spot each state gets.

VINAY Bhat 14 YEARS OLD

Born in California, June 4, 1984

At the age of 14, Vinay Bhat of San Jose, California, has already won the Pan American Championship (Under-14), US Cadet Championship (Under-16) and earned a Bronze Medal in the World Boys Under-12 Championship in 1996.

He is the United States representative at the 1998 World Boys Under-14 Championship which will be held in Spain later this year.

Vinay came to the attention of the chess world back in 1991, when he won the National 2nd Grade Championship at the age of seven. The next year he won the 3rd Grade Championship, and in 1993 was the overall winner of the National Elementary Schools Speed Chess Championship. That year he also became the youngest National Master in American chess history. He made his international debut in 1994, tying for 6th place at the World Boys Under-10 Championship in Szeged, Hungary. The following year he improved significantly, and tied for second at the World Boys Under-12 Championship in Brazil. He also won the Aspis Award as the best chess player under-13 in the US.

In 1995 television cameras recorded Vinay's victory in the Chessmaster Youth Challenge, where he and fellow whiz kids Jordy Mont-Reynaud and Jennie Frenklakh competed against each other and the Chessmaster computer program at the Pan Pacific International. 1996 saw Vinay harvest a bumper crop, include the bronze medal in Spain, the US Open Master Blitz Championship, and the National Junior High School Championship. The medal was especially welcome, since in 1995 Bhat tied for second place, losing the medal on tie-breaks.

He also set a record by becoming the youngest American ever to win an official

Vinay is in the Guinness Book of World Records!

game against a Grandmaster (the highest level of chess player). He also tied for second at the World Rapid Chess (Boys Under-12) Championship in France. In 1997, Vinay started his adjustment to professional chess, competing in the Hawaii International and winning the Inland Empire Open. He represented the US in the World Boys Under-14 Championship but did not bring home a medal in this very tough competition. This year he won the Pan American Boys Under-14 and finished second in the Denker Tournament of High School Champions, even though he just enters high school in the fall!

For his victory in the Pan American Championship he was awarded the title of FIDE Master. He now sets his sights on the title of International Master, for which he must earn about 200 ranking points and also meet qualification requirements in at least three events. He has achieved his success without a great deal of training. His mother, Vijaya, has been the major chess influence and she is a pretty good player herself. Usually it is the father who provides early chess instruction, but Vinay's dad is the only non-chessplayer in the family!

Chess is not the only area in which Vinay excels. He has won awards for science, story writing and sports. In fact, he doesn't even train regularly in chess. Vinay prefers to learn from his mistakes, and doesn't put in the hours of study which are a normal part of most top young player's days. When it comes to opening theory, he admits to being a little lazy. Fortunately, his ability has carried him so far that it is hard to argue with his success!

There are many different kinds of prizes in chess. Sometimes money is the reward, sometimes trophies, sometimes just honor and glory. At the World Youth Festival in Menorca, Spain, in 1996, Vinay got a special reward for winning the Bronze Medal in the World Boys Under-12 Championship. He got to push his coach (your author) into the swimming pool fully clothed! A photographer was on hand to capture the moment.

Eric takes a dip, courtesy of Vinay Bhat

ONE OF MY BEST GAMES SO FAR

Vinay has played many exciting games, and selected this as among his best. It was played in one of the most important American tournaments, the New York Open. Every year over a thousand chessplayers congregate in New York to compete for over $150,000. The large cash prizes lead to no mercy on the part of the strongest players, and most games are long battles. Many young players, including Irina, opted for the section restricted to players rated under-2400, but Vinay (and your author) boldly stepped into the top section. Against Colombia's Carlos Perdomo, who is playing in his national championship as this is being written, Vinay showed he was up to the competition.

VINAY VS. PERDOMO
New York Open 1998

1.e4 c5; 2.Nf3 Nc6; 3.Bb5 g6; 4.Bxc6 dxc6; 5.h3 Bg7; 6.d3 Nf6.

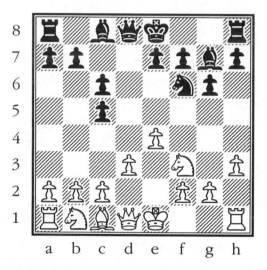

This was my first time facing this system where Black didn't advance the e-pawn to d5. So I had to improvise a bit. **7.Nc3 0-0; 8.0-0 b6; 9.Bg5!?** My bishop will be driven back, but my opponent must weaken his kingside to do so.

9...h6; 10.Be3 Kh7; 11.a4 Qc7; 12.Nd2 e5; 13.f4 Nh5? My opponent either had not seen my next move, or he had underestimated it. He should have taken my f-pawn instead, even though I might have been able to take advantage of an empty e5-square. 13...exf4; 14.Bxf4 Qe7; 15.Nc4 Ne8; 16.e5!? Be6; 17.Ne4 Bxc4; 18.dxc4 is better for me, as I could attack on the kingside for example 18...Nc7?!; 19.Nf6+ Kh8; 20.Qd2 Rad8; 21.Qe3 h5; 22.Bg5 when Black has a lot to worry about.

14.f5 Nf4; 15.g3! I saw this move very quickly. I wanted to get rid of the knight and alternatives didn't seem that good to me.

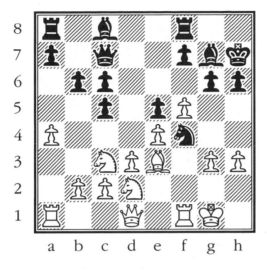

15...Nh5. The pawn at h3 could not be captured safely. 15...Nxh3+; 16.Kg2 Now the retreat 16...Ng5 loses to a complicated line. 17.Bxg5 hxg5; 18.f6 Bh6 (18...Bh8; 19.Rh1+ Kg8; 20.Rxh8+ Kxh8; 21.Qh1+ Kg8; 22.Qh6 forces checkmate.); 19.Rh1 Qd7 Here I have a number of winning plans, but one nice clean one is 20.Rh2 Rh8; 21.Qh1 Kg8; 22.Rxh6 Rxh6; 23.Qxh6 and Black must give up a piece with 23...Qh3+; 24.Qxh3 Bxh3+; 25.Kxh3 which is an easy win. No better is 16...gxf5; 17.exf5 (17.Kxh3?? would lose to 17...f4+) 17...Ng5 (17...Nf4+; 18.gxf4 Rg8; 19.Qh5 exf4 looks like it gives Black some chances, but after 20.Nde4! The threat is 21.Ng5+; 22.Nxcf7+; 23.Qg6#.

Black can take my knight with discovered check, and then take my bishop, but even then I am better. 20...Bxc3+; 21.Kf3 fxe3; 22.Rh1. Threatens Qh6# but if Black defends by retreating the bishop I win with the plan mentioned above 22...Bg7; 23.Ng5+ Kh8; 24.Nxf7+ Black must sacrifice the queen because of the threat of mate at g6. 24...Qxf7; 25.Qxf7 Rf8; 26.Qc4 Bxf5; 27.Kxe3 gives me a queen for two bishops and a pawn which is pretty weak.); 18.Bxg5 hxg5; 19.Qh5+ Bh6 (19...Kg8 gets mated by 20.f6 Bh8; 21.Qxg5+ Kh7; 22.Rh1+ Bh3+; 23.Rxh3#); 20.Rh1 Qd6; 21.Nde4 I win.

So, my opponent chose the best plan. I have a small edge, but nothing much. **16.Qf3 Rg8; 17.Ne2.** I wanted to play g4, but didn't worry about Black sacrificing a pawn with Nf4 to get dark-square play.

Vinay won the Aspis Award as the best chess player under-13 in the US, and followed that up by winning the Pan American Championship (Under-14).

17...Nf6; 18.g4 Bd7; 19.Kf2 Rad8; 20.Ng3.

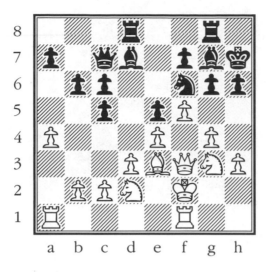

20...Bc8. 20...gxf5; 21.Nxf5 Bxf5; 22.Qxf5+ Kh8; 23.Bxh6 Bxh6; 24.Qxf6+ Kh7; 25.Qf5+ is very bad for Black. **21.Rh1 Bh8; 22.Rag1.** White slowly prepares the breakthrough on the kingside as there is no counterplay for Black in the center.

22...Qe7; 23.h4 Ne8. 23...Nxg4+?; 24.Qxg4 gxf5 threatens to play ...f4 and win back the piece, but I have a counterstrike. 25.Nxf5! Rxg4; 26.Nxe7 keeps the extra piece. 23...gxf5 doesn't work either. 24.Nxf5 Bxf5; 25.Qxf5+ Kg7; 26.Bxh6+ Kxh6; 27.g5+ Kg7; 28.gxf6+ Kf8; 29.Rxg8+ Kxg8; 30.fxe7 wins. **24.g5 Nd6.** 24...h5 lets me play 25.Nxh5 since 25...gxh5 gets mated by 26.Qxh5+ Kg7; 27.Qh6#; **25.f6 Qe6.**

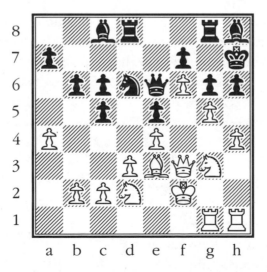

Black has no counterplay. **26.h5.** The pawns crash through no matter what Black does. **26...Qg4; 27.hxg6+ Rxg6; 28.Qxg4 Bxg4; 29.Rh4 Be6; 30.Nf3 c4.** Black can't guard the e-pawn. **31.Nxe5 cxd3.** 31...Rgg8?? would have ended the game instantly with 32.Rxh6#; **32.cxd3 Kg8; 33.Rgh1 Bb3; 34.Nf5 Bxf6.** My idea was 34...Bxa4; 35.Ne7+ Kf8; 36.N5xg6+ fxg6; 37.Nxg6+ Kf7; 38.Rxh6 winning the bishop. **35.Nxg6 Nxf5; 36.exf5 hxg5.**

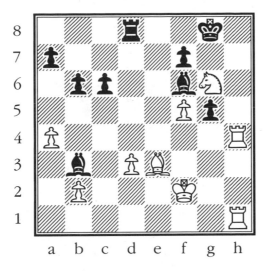

The end was amusing. **37.Rh8+!** Black resigns. 37...Kg7 runs into 38.R1h7# but 37...Bxh8; 38.Rxh8+ Kg7; 39.Rxd8 fxg6; 40.Bd4+ Kf7; 41.f6 leaves me a whole rook up and I will win the enemy bishop, which will have to sacrifice itself to keep my f-pawn from promoting.

Vinay wins!

JENNIE *Frenklakh* 18 YEARS OLD

Born on May 4, 1980 in Mozyr, Belarus.

Jennie has been involved with chess from an early age, even before she came to America. She enters Boston University this year as a 1998 Scholar Chessplayer, a scholarship awarded by the United States Chess Federation. As with most of the talented young players on the West Coast, she has not had intensive training with any one person, but has absorbed knowledge from her father, a chess and Russian language teacher, and a number of tutors. Jennie has received a lot of attention, and made the front page of the San Francisco Examiner when she had a fantastic start at the 1995 US Open, accompanied by a stuffed bear that served as a good luck charm.

"My dad taught me the game when I was four years old. I played my first tournament when I was 6. It was held in the city of Minsk. I was too short to reach across the board, so I had to sit on a few large books and briefcases. I constantly forgot to press the clock, so my dad wrote "TIME" in big letters on my score sheet before the game. I got an even score of 2.5/5 and received a tiny chess set as a prize for being the youngest and most promising player of the tournament.

"I have been given the honor and privilege of representing the U.S. at six World Youth and Junior Championships. It has been a great learning experience, both in life and in chess. It has given me the opportunity to travel all around Europe, meet many fascinating people and learn chess from some of the greatest players in the world. I've been lucky enough to have played in many countries, including Russia, Belarus, Germany, Slovakia, Hungary, Spain, Poland and all over the United States.

Being invited to the U.S. Women's Invitational Championship three times and earning the title of a national master are also some of my most significant accomplishments.

> *Jennie holds the prestigious title of National Master*

"I enjoy playing volleyball and swimming. I also like spending time with my friends, going to the movies, amusement parks, bowling. I also spend time educating kids in chess. I've taught at elementary schools, camps, and have designed an interactive chess website called Chess Dominion (http://library.advanced.org/10746).

"Chess is a very unique game. Unlike most other games, no two chess games ever repeat themselves and the player is required to use his or her brain in order to outsmart the opponent. Chess teaches you patience, and to look both ways before crossing the street. It is a very just game, where mistakes are punished and hard work is rewarded. Chess allows me to travel to many exciting places, meet interesting people and make lifelong friendships. This is why I don't see the day when I stop playing this game."

ONE OF MY BEST GAMES SO FAR

This game is characteristic of Jennie's "new" style. In the past, she had played without much ambition in the opening, but starting in 1996 she adopted a much more aggressive set of openings. Where she used to timidly deploy her pieces in safe positions, she now hurls them at her opponent, even sacrificing pawns in the opening! In last year's world championship for girls under 20, she faced strong opposition throughout. Here, her opponent selects the treacherous Modern Benoni Defense, and Jennie takes up the challenge, playing White's most aggressive line.

JENNIE VS. AROUCHE
World Junior Girls Championship, Zagan, Poland, 1997

1.d4 Nf6; 2.c4 c5; 3.d5 e6; 4.Nc3 exd5; 5.cxd5 d6; 6.e4 g6; 7.f4.

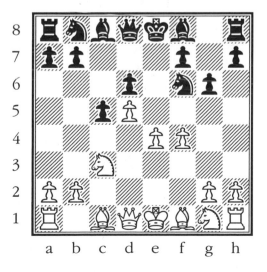

All this is well known theory, and both players were prepared. **7...Bg7; 8.Bb5+ Nfd7; 9.a4 0–0; 10.Nf3 Na6; 11.0–0 Nc7; 12.Bxd7.** White can retreat the bishop but that concedes an equal game. **12...Bxd7; 13.f5!?** A popular sacrifice, it seems, because it was repeated twice in 1998.

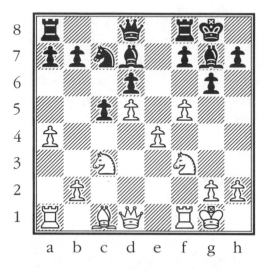

13...a6 My opponent decides to decline the gambit. 13...gxf5 leads to an interesting game after 14.Bg5 f6; 15.Bf4 where Black has not been able to equalize.

15...Ne8 (15...Re8; 16.exf5 Bxf5; 17.Nh4 forces the bishop to retreat and the weakness of the kingside and passive Black knight at c7 give White more than enough compensation for the pawn in Houska vs. Tebb, Torquay 1998.); 16.Qd2 a6; 17.h3 b5; 18.axb5 axb5; 19.Rxa8 Qxa8; 20.exf5 Bxf5; 21.Nxb5 with Black suffering from poorly placed pieces in Giorgadze against Kovacevic, Ubeda 1998.

> *J*enny represented the U.S. at six World Youth and Junior Championships and earned a Scholar Chessplayer scholarship to Boston University!

14.Bg5 f6. 14...Bf6 offers an exchange of bishops, but the strongest reply is 15.Bh6 Re8; 16.fxg6; **15.Bf4 Qe7; 16.fxg6 hxg6; 17.Nh4 Kf7.** 17...g5?? loses to 18.Ng6 Qf7; 19.Nxf8 gxf4; 20.Nxd7 Qxd7; 21.Rxf4 with an overwhelming advantage.

18.Qd3 Rg8.

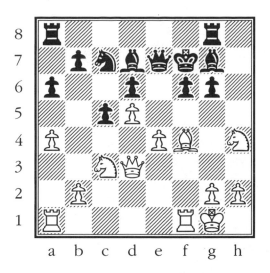

Black has four pieces covering e5, so surely that square is safe. **19.e5!** This opens up a discovered attack on the weak pawn at g6. **19...dxe5; 20.Qxg6+ Kf8; 21.Qd3.** The queen retreats to a safer square. There is a threatened knight fork at g6. **21...Be8; 22.Rae1!** A successful attack needs all the pieces. This move also adds a direct threat of Bxe5. **22...Bf7.** Blocks the file, but there is a small tactical problem. **23.Bxe5!**

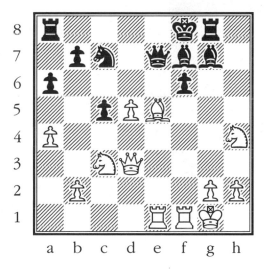

Black cannot capture the bishop with the pawn because of Ng6+; the bishop at f7 would be pinned by the rook at f1. **23...Qd8; 24.d6 Qd7.** The knight is taboo because the d-pawn is pinned to the queen at d3. White settles for the f-pawn, an important defender of the king. **25.Bxf6 Bxf6; 26.Rxf6 Ne8.** White is winning, and uses an efficient sacrifice to win more material. **27.Rxf7+! Qxf7; 28.Rf1 Nf6.** Forced, to protect the queen, which is pinned. **29.Ne4 Kg7; 30.Nxf6.** The rest is just mopping up. **30...Kh8; 31.Nxg8 Qxg8; 32.Qf5 Qg7; 33.Ng6+ Kg8; 34.Ne7+ Kh8; 35.Rf4.**

MATTHEW HO 10 YEARS OLD

Born May 22, 1988, San Jose California

Matthew Ho of San Jose, California is the latest prodigy to emerge from the West Coast. He started playing in 1994 and entered his first tournament in the 2nd Annual Scholastic Chess Conference 1996, at the age of six, earning first place in the Under-700 category.

Matthew quickly rose through the rating ranks. He scored an amazing 5 out of 7 in the National High School Championships in May, 1998. Matthew qualified to participate in the World Boys Under-10 Championship in October, 1998 in the Spanish town of Oropesa de Mar. This will be his first tournament abroad.

Matthew attends Faria Elementary School. When not playing chess, he enjoys other computer games. In the summer of 1998 he started training with Eric Schiller.

At the 1998 Cardoza US Open he had many strong players on the ropes, but was not able to take advantage of all his opportunities. He finished with 4 points out of 9, a very respectable score for a 10-year old!

> *I like chess because it is a fun game. It also makes you the think and helps in math problem solving. Chess is an educational game, and it is played seriously around the world.*

ONE OF MY BEST GAMES SO FAR

I won a brilliancy prize for this game, so it is definitely my favorite! My opponent was higher rated by over a hundred points and got to move first, but I played well to win.

CALONIA VS. MATTHEW
LERA Memorial Day, Sunnyvale CA, 1998

1.d4 d5; 2.e3 Nf6; 3.Bd3 c5; 4.c3 Nc6; 5.f4 Bg4; 6.Nf3 e6; 7.0-0 Bd6.

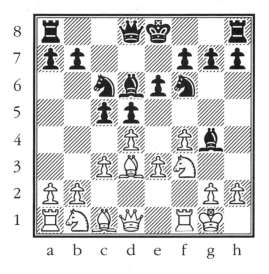

White plays a Stonewall Attack. The idea is to set up an attacking formation. Matthew has set up a good defense and will soon surprise his opponent by castling on the queenside. **8.Qe1 Qc7; 9.Ne5 Bh5; 10.Nd2 0-0-0; 11.a4 Nd7; 12.Qg3 f6; 13.Nxc6 Qxc6; 14.Qxg7 Rdg8.**

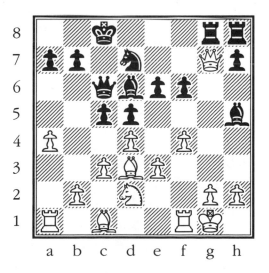

The pawn sacrifice opens up a line directly into the enemy camp. **15.Qh6 Bg6; 16.Bb5.** 16.Bxg6 hxg6 traps the White queen! **16...Qc7; 17.Qh4 Be7; 18.Qh3 Bf5; 19.Qf3 h5.** The h-pawn is not really used for attack, but to gain some maneuvering space for Black on the kingside. **20.e4 Bg4.** 20...dxe4; 21.Nxe4 Bxe4; 22.Qxe4 is just what White wants.

21.Qe3 cxd4; 22.cxd4 Nb6. It is a good thing White cannot get a rook to c1 to pin the Black queen!; **23.h3.**

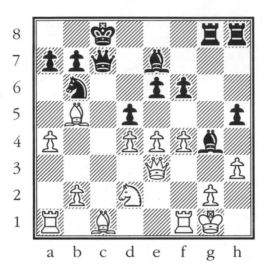

White should have pushed the a-pawn instead. Matthew is prepared to sacrifice the bishop on the kingside, because that will open up even more lines. Matthew's next move is truly superb, expertly calculated and worthy of any master.

23...e5!! As a practical matter, the advance of the e-pawn creates numerous threats. Black attacks all three central pawns. White must be particularly careful not to move the pawn from d4, because Black can play ...Bc5 and pin the White queen to the king.

24.fxe5 fxe5; 25.a5. Too late! This should have been played instead of 23.h3. 25.hxg4 exd4; 26.Qf2 (26.Qxd4 loses the queen to 26...Bc5) 26...hxg4 threatens ...Qh2#. 27.e5 is a little trick.

If Black takes the pawn, then White gets to exchange queens. 27...Qxe5 (27...g3; 28.Qf5+ Kb8; 29.Nf3 Rf8; 30.Qd3 Rh5 keeps the attack alive. Does Black have enough for the piece? That is not clear.

As a practical matter, White must worry about the long term

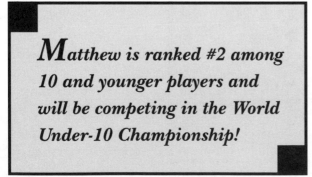

*M*atthew is ranked #2 among 10 and younger players and will be competing in the World Under-10 Championship!

safety of his king and Black needs a few moves for development. Activating the rooks will be particularly difficult. Even if they double on the c-file, they don't constitute a major threat.); 28.Qf5+ Qxf5; 29.Rxf5 and White has a big advantage.

25...exd4; 26.axb6. Greedy. 26.Qb3 would have taken the initiative. **26...dxe3; 27.bxc7 exd2; 28.Bxd2.**

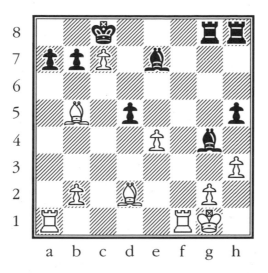

Perhaps White had seen this far, counting on winning the pawn at d5 even if the c-pawn falls. There were still problems on the kingside, however. **28...Bxh3!** The bishop cannot be captured because the pawn at g2 is pinned by the Black rook. **29.Rf2.** The only way to defend g2, but there is another pin! **29...Bc5!; 30.Rc1 Rxg2+!; 31.Kh1 Bxf2; 32.cxd5.**

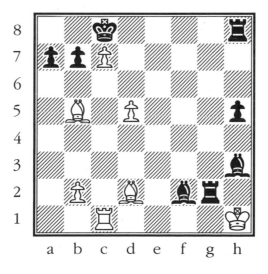

The armies are at equal strength, but Black's king is completely safe, thanks to the bishop at h3. The White king is doomed.

32...Rhg8. 32...Bg3 would have been more efficient, but Matthew saw a clear path to the win and followed it. 33.Rc3 Rh2+; 34.Kg1 Be5; 35.Rxh3 Rg8+; 36.Kf1 Rxh3 gives Black a pile of extra material, and White's pawns are not at all dangerous.

33.d6 Rg1+; 34.Rxg1 Rxg1+; 35.Kh2 Bd7. Black has an extra rook, and the pawns are stopped in their tracks. Resignation would have been appropriate here.

36.Be2 Bc6; 37.d7+ Kxd7; 38.c8Q+ Kxc8. Faced with mate in three, White resigned.

GABE *Kahane* 17 YEARS OLD

Born in Venice, California, July 10, 1981

Santa Rosa's Gabe Kahane spent most of his early childhood in Rochester, New York, before returning to the West Coast in 1995 to live in Santa Rosa, California. His father, a concert pianist and conductor, taught him chess at the age of four, but it was not until Gabe was nine that he began to play chess seriously.

In Rochester, under the instruction of Senior Master Isay Golyak, he became a USCF expert at the age of thirteen. After moving to Santa Rosa, he met your author, with whom he still studies. His titles include equal first with National Master Steve Winer at the 1993 U.S. Junior Chess Congress East and 1997 California State Scholastic Blitz Champion.

His best achievement to date is a third place tie at the 1998 National High School Championship, where he held the top seed to a draw and gave up only one other draw.

Although Gabe intends on pursuing chess as a part of his life, he is also interested in music, particularly jazz and choral music, and very involved in theater. Gabe sings and plays guitar in a "folk-bluesy-rock" band (Typical Daydream) and is a fan of the Dave Matthews Band.

Gabe attends Santa Rosa High School and Santa Rosa Junior College and hopes to proceed with further education on the East Coast after his graduation from high school. His recent acquisition of a driver's license will enable him to play in more tournaments.

Although he has played under top conditions in Germany, Hawaii, and all over the mainland America, Gabe knows that tournament life is

> *Gabe won the 1993 U.S. Junior Chess Congress East and 1997 California State Scholastic Blitz Championship.*

not always a first class affair.

"Eating after a late round always presents a problem. Very often, the hotel restaurants are closed, and the nearest open restaurants are far from walking distance. One night at the US Masters in Chicago saw eleven young chess players quite hungry after an evening round, and with only one car, a Herculean task would follow. As it turned out, Jason Doss, Jim Dean, Greg Shahade, Jennie Frenklakh, Charles Gelman, Andrei Zaremba, Jeff Ashton, Todd Andrews, John Bick, Ryan Mankaweics and I were all crammed into a car that was meant to seat only five!

"One can only imagine how uncomfortable that was, especially with the reward being a mediocre meal at Denny's!"

ONE OF MY BEST GAMES SO FAR

HEYL VS. GABE
Outrigger Prince Kuhio International, Honolulu, 1997

1.d4 d5; 2.Nf3 e6; 3.c4 c5; 4.cxd5 exd5; 5.Nc3 Nc6; 6.g3 Nf6; 7.Bg2 Be7; 8.0–0 0–0. This is the Classical Tarrasch Defense. I had been studying it a lot. **9.Bg5 cxd4; 10.Nxd4 h6; 11.Be3 Re8; 12.Rc1 Bf8; 13.a3.**

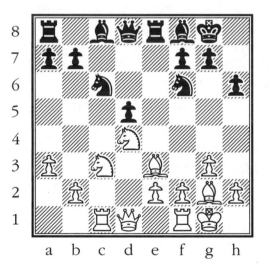

Up to this point we have been following well known chess theory and I didn't have to think of any new moves. My opponent tried a new move by advancing the a-pawn, but fooling around on the flank was not correct. He should have concentrated on the center of the board, capturing my knight at c6 and then bringing his remaining knight to c5, via a4.

13...Bg4; 14.Re1 Qd7; 15.Nxc6 bxc6; 16.Na4 At last he finds the appropriate plan, but it is too late, because I am ready to attack on the kingside. **16...Bh3!;**

17.Bf3? This is just a waste of time, and the bishop just retreats back to g2 on the next turn.

17...Ne4; 18.Bg2 Bxg2; 19.Kxg2 Re5 I wanted to cut his throat with a brutal attack on the kingside. **20.h3?** Another mistake, and this time it is fatal. The weakness at g3 lets me win nicely.

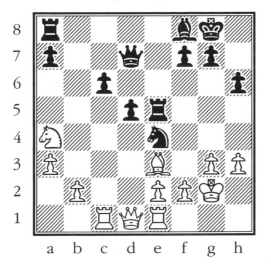

20...Nxg3; 21.Kxg3. 21.fxg3 Rxe3 is hopeless for White. **21...Qd6.** For the sacrificed piece I have a tremendous attack, with the threat of discovered check when my rook moves.

22.Kg2. 22.Bf4 is more complicated. 22...Rg5+; 23.Kf3 Rf5 (23...Qg6 was my idea, but Eric pointed out that 24.Bxg5 Qe4+; 25.Kg3 Bd6+; 26.f4 hxg5; 27.e3 gxf4+; 28.Kf2 leaves me with no way to continue the attack, and the two pawns are not worth as much as White's extra piece.) 24.e3 g5 wins back the piece. 25.Qd3 Qf6; 26.Rg1 Bg7 and Black will emerge with the advantage, according to analysis by Eric. 27.Rxc6 Rxf4+!; 28.exf4 Qxc6; 29.fxg5 hxg5; 30.Nc3 d4+; 31.Qe4 Qc8!

> *I am a faithful Najdorf player due to my obsession with messy positions, as well as the fact that I am able to get advantages out of the opening against even the strongest players if I am able to out-theory them.*

Material is even, but the pawn at h3 is under attack, as is the knight at c3. White can't save both.

22...Qg6+; 23.Kh2.

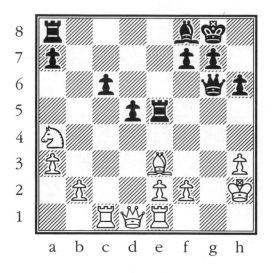

23...Rxe3! A final sacrifice brings home the point. **24.Rc3** Or 24.fxe3 Bd6+; 25.Kh1 Qg3 followed by mate at h2. **24...Bd6+; 25.Kh1 Qe4+; 26.Kg1;** 26.f3 Qf4 also leads to checkmate. **26...Qf4.** White resigned this hopeless position.

IRINA *Krush* 14 YEARS OLD

Born 24 December 1983, Ukraine, USSR

*I*t didn't take long for Irina Krush to make an impact on the American chess scene. She arrived in Brooklyn, where she now lives, at the age of eight, and earned her National Master title from the United States Chess Federation at twelve. She is already a veteran of the United States Women's Championship (her first appearance in this invitational event came when she was just 11!), and qualified for the United States Olympiad team in 1998.

Under the supervision of her trainer, Mikhail Trosman, and informal help from Grandmaster Ron Henley she has been able to make tremendous progress and is already the highest ranked woman under the age of twenty. She also benefits greatly from the sponsorship of the WWW Chess Superstore.

An unmistakable presence at any chess tournament, Irina Krush has already survived the pressure of international competition at the highest level. The 1998 Pan American Girls Under-14 Champion is on a record breaking pace to become the youngest American woman star.

Irina has been a chessplayer for a long time. At the age of 9 she defeated a National Master in a record-breaking performance. She has participated in many World Youth Championships, but has been a bit unlucky there. Irina won the Silver Medal at the Eurodisney Rapid Championships in 1996, and took Gold at the Pan American Girls this year. Skipping the World Girls Under-16, she is aiming for higher goals

> *A*t the age of 14, Irina was already the highest ranked U.S. woman under the age of 20!

and will compete in the US Women's Championship instead. Then she will move up and try for the World Junior Girls Championship in India this December.

Krush is already making the transition from youth competitions to professional chess. She plays regular exhibition matches against Grandmasters. This year she held Grandmaster Arthur Bisguier, a former United States Champion, to a draw in a four game contest, and narrowly lost to John Fedorowicz, who was one of her coaches at the Pan American Championships.

Irina doesn't just play chess, she also writes about the game and has her own set of instructional videos, "Krushing Attacks." She is a columnist for SmartChess Online and her articles have also appeared in *Chess Life* and *Atlantic Chess News*.

One of the most emotional chessplayers, Irina can rarely conceal her feelings after a game. When she lost the second game against Bisguier, Irina said "I want to curl up into a ball and just die." The next game was a victory, and now all she had to say was, "Yippee!". We'll see that game a little later on. Let's start with an appetizer from one of her recent tournaments.

ONE OF MY BEST GAMES

This game was played in Hawaii at the Cardoza US Open. It has a lot of nice tactics. My opponent is a former President of the United States Chess Federation.

IRINA VS. REDMAN
Cardoza US Open, Kona, Hawaii, 1998

1.d4 g6; 2.e4 c6; 3.Nc3 d5.

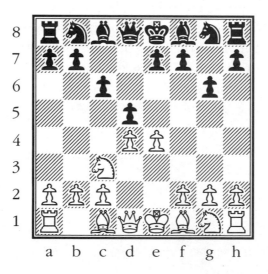

Black chooses a solid system which leaves him a little cramped. The Gurgenidze Defense is notoriously tough to crack, and White must play patiently.

4.Nf3 Bg4; 5.Be2 Bg7; 6.exd5 cxd5; 7.Ne5! The exchange of light-squared bishops favors White, because the g4 bishop is Black's only developed piece.

7...Bxe2; 8.Qxe2 Qa5; 9.0–0 Nc6. Black reckons that an exchange at c6 would open up the b-file and help shore up the d-pawn.

10.Nb5 Nxe5. Krush had a tremendous threat of Nd6+, for example 10...Nf6; 11.Nd6+ Kf8 (11...exd6; 12.Nxc6+ wins Black's queen because of the check on the e-file.); 12.Ndxf7 Rg8; 13.Nxc6 bxc6; 14.Nh6 leaves Black a pawn behind with a miserable position.

11.dxe5 a6; 12.Nd4 e6.

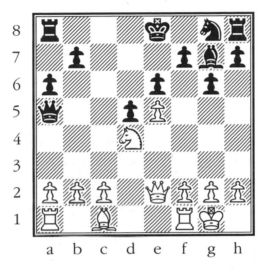

Black has a solid pawn at d5 but has not castled and there are now serious weaknesses on the kingside dark squares, which Krush exploits mercilessly.

13.Bg5 Qb6; 14.c3 h6; 15.Bh4 Qc7; 16.f4 Ne7; 17.Qg4! The queen is in an excellent attacking position. Perhaps Black should nevertheless castle on the kingside, instead of weakening the dark squares further by advancing the h-pawn.

17...h5?!; 18.Qg5! Bf8 18...Nc6 would have been better. **19.Qg3 Ng8.** Black has returned the minor pieces to their home squares. Although material is even, White controls so much space that Black starts to suffocate.

20.Rad1 Bc5.

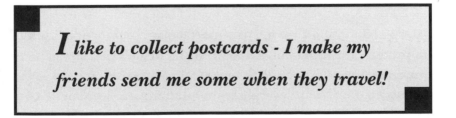

I like to collect postcards - I make my friends send me some when they travel!

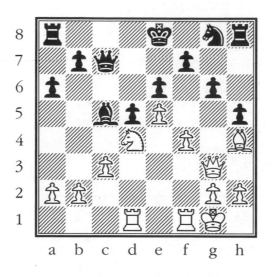

Black plans to get rid of the pesky knight once and for all. The knight seems to be necessary to support any advance of the f-pawn.

21.f5! A fine move which rips open Black's protective armor. **21...exf5.** 21...gxf5; 22.Qg7 wins at least a piece. **22.Rxf5! Nh6.** The sacrifice cannot be accepted: 22...gxf5; 23.Qg7 Rh6; 24.Qxg8+ Kd7; 25.Qxf7+ Be7; 26.Qxe7+ Kc8; 27.Qe8+ Qd8; 28.Qxd8#. **23.Rf4.**

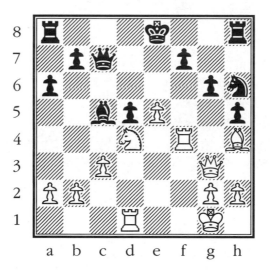

23...0-0. 23...Nf5 would have led to a spectacular combination. 24.Rxf5!! gxf5; 25.Qg7 Rf8 protects the rook, but 26.e6! destroys Black's position. The pawn cannot be captured because it is pinned to the queen. The position is very complicated and the analysis could take up several pages, but here are two sample conclusions.

26...Qf4 is best, and White must find good moves. (26...Bxd4+ gets rid of the knight but the e-pawn reaches e7 and the rook has nowhere to run. 27.Rxd4 Qc5;

28.e7 Kd7; 29.exf8Q Rxf8; 30.Qe5 is resignable.); 27.Qf6! A hard move to find, but it creates serious problems for Black because of the threat of the advance of the e-pawn. Black can try defending by checking, moving the queen to the e-file, or attacking the rook but they all fail. 27...Qe3+ (27...Qe4 invites disaster after 28.Re1!

27...Qg4; 28.Re1 also creates unstoppable threats of capture at f7 and infiltration by the rook, for example 28...f4; 29.exf7+ Kd7; 30.h3 which traps the Black queen!); 28.Kh1 fxe6 (28...Bxd4 allows checkmate with 29.Qe7#); 29.Qxe6+ Qxe6; 30.Nxe6. The formerly pinned knight reigns supreme, threatening the rook at f8, bishop at c5, and a fork at c7. 30...Bb6; 31.Nxf8 Kxf8; 32.Rxd5 picks off both kingside pawns with an easy win. Castling only delayed the inevitable.

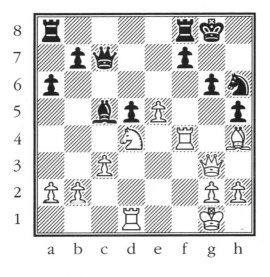

24.Bf6 Kh7; 25.Rh4 Nf5. Black seems to have some major threats here.

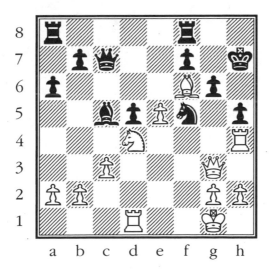

Black threatens both queen and rook, but Irina is prepared with an ambitious sacrifice.

26.Rxh5+!! gxh5. Forced, or mate comes quickly.

27.Qd3 Qd7; 28.Rf1 Kg6. Black is hanging on to all the pieces. **29.h3.** The direct threat of advancing the pawn to g4 was the most efficient way of wrapping up the game, but for sheer beauty there was the alternative 29.Rxf5, which forces 29...Bxd4+ with the cute reply 30.Rf2+! An unpin and discovered check! 30...Kh6; 31.Qxd4 with a very strong attack and weak Black pawns to use for target practice.

29...Rg8. Not the best defense. 29...Bxd4+; 30.cxd4 h4 prevents White from playing g4. 31.Qd2 returns to the dark squares. 31...Kh7; 32.Qg5 leaves Black with only one defense to mate. 32...Rg8 (32...Rac8; 33.Rxf5 Rc1+; 34.Kh2 and either 35.Qg7 or 35.Qh5 will finish the job.); 33.Qxf5+ Qxf5; 34.Rxf5 and the h-pawn will fall. The bishop and extra pawns are worth more than the enemy rook. Still, Black would have had some chances to hang on.

30.g4. 30.Rxf5 still works. 30...Bxd4+; 31.Rf2+ Kh6; 32.Qxd4 does allow 32...Qxh3 but 33.Qd2+ Kh7; 34.Qc2+ Rg6 (34...Kh6; 35.Bg7+! Rxg7; 36.Rf6+ Rg6; 37.Rxg6+ fxg6; 38.gxh3 is similar.); 35.Qxg6+ fxg6; 36.gxh3 and White has an easy win.

30...Kh7. 30...Bxd4+; 31.cxd4 hxg4; 32.hxg4 Kh7 almost escapes, but not quite. 33.Rxf5! Rxg4+; 34.Kf2 Kg8; 35.Rh5 etc. **31.Rxf5.** Black resigned. The position is hopeless.

Irina and Hikaru discuss it at the board

JORDY Mont-Reynaud

15 YEARS OLD

Born August 16, 1983 in Palo Alto, California

Jordy Mont-Reynaud catapulted to national attention in 1994, when he became the youngest master in American Chess at the age of ten. At the time, the Mont-Reynauds were renting a home belonging to the sister of the great Bobby Fischer, who won the World Championship in 1972 against Russian Boris Spassky! Fischer himself used to stay in the house, so it was filled with inspiration for the aspiring player.

Jordy was brought into scholastic chess by Alan Fischer-Kirschner, a major scholastic chess organizer in the Bay Area. He spotted Jordy playing at a local library when Mont-Reynaud was just six years old. With early training by National Master Lee Corbin, and author Major Bill Wall, he quickly learned strategy and tactics.

Jordy started to earn chess honors in 1989, finishing in tenth place in the California primary school championships. He continued to progress, and won the Silver medal at the 1993 World Youth Championships. He received additional instruction from noted trainers and Grandmasters, including Lev Alburt, Mark Dvoretsky, Roman Dzindzichashvili, Gabe Sanchez, Eric Schiller, and Dmitry Zernitsky.

Jordy is busy as a top student at Gunn High School, but still finds time for tennis, soccer, photography and music. He is an accomplished musician who has performed as soloist and with local orchestras. He enjoys aquatic sports, and discovered boogie-boarding while competing in the Hawaii International tournaments.

> *A*t the age of 10, Jordy became the youngest player ever to achieve the USCF Master title, achieving a rating of 2212!

He speaks French well, and is studying Hebrew in preparation for his Bar Mitzvah. How does he find time for all this?

Perhaps the intentional lack of television in the Mont-Reynaud home accounts for that! Fortunately for Jordy (or not), traveling to chess tournaments provides access to that form of popular culture. In any case, he doesn't let chess get in the way of his other interests. As he once said, "If I played all the time, I wouldn't have time to play ping pong!"

ONE OF MY BEST GAMES SO FAR

Jordy displays an acute awareness of action on both sides of the board in this impressive win at the World Open, when he was just 11 years old. The winning plan is very sophisticated!

JORDY VS. BUCKS
World Open, Philadelphia, 1995

1.d4 Nf6; 2.c4 g6; 3.Nc3 Bg7; 4.e4 d6; 5.Be2 0-0; 6.Bg5 c5; 7.d5 h6; 8.Be3 e5; 9.Qd2 Kh7.

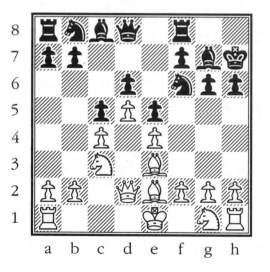

Even as a candidate master Jordy was comfortable following the main lines of opening theory, in this case the Averbakh Variation of the King's Indian Defense.

10.h4 Na6; 11.a3. Jordy shows some patience, not rushing the kingside attack. Instead, he anticipates his opponent's play on the other side of the board. He is confident that the kingside opportunities will remain. In the King's Indian, Black often attacks on the kingside, so White must play vigorously on the queenside. By taking over the queenside, Jordy forces his opponent to open up the kingside, or risk getting crushed on the opposite flank.

11...Ne8; 12.h5 g5; 13.Qd1 Nac7; 14.b4 b6; 15.Rb1 Kg8; 16.Bd3 f5.

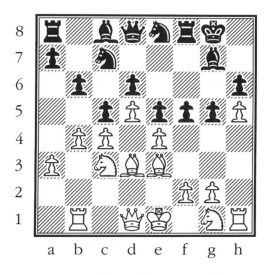

There was nothing better, but now there are holes in Black's position, especially at g6, which plays a crucial role in the final combination. **17.exf5 Bxf5; 18.Bxf5 Rxf5; 19.Qd3 Rf7; 20.Nge2.** The weakness of Black's light squares is obvious. The bishop at g7 is relegated to a purely defensive role. **20...Nf6; 21.Ng3 Ng4; 22.0-0 cxb4; 23.axb4 Qd7; 24.c5! bxc5; 25.bxc5 Nxe3.**

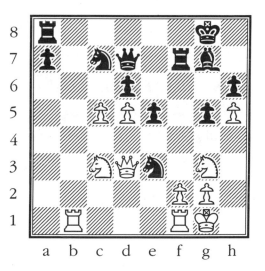

Black had to get rid of this bishop, and perhaps expected White to capture immediately. Instead, Jordy ignores the knight and attacks the enemy queen, establishing a passed pawn and an outpost on b7 for the rook.

26.c6! Qg4; 27.Qxe3 Qd4; 28.Nge4! White is happy to exchange queens and enter an endgame with the powerful passed c-pawn. Black declines. **28...Bf8; 29.Rb7 a5; 30.Rd1 Qc4; 31.Qb6!**

A beautiful move. The attack on the knight is a clever way of repositioning the queen, which will take up a position on the b1–h7 diagonal.

31...Ra6; 32.Qb1! Ne8; 33.Rxf7 Kxf7.

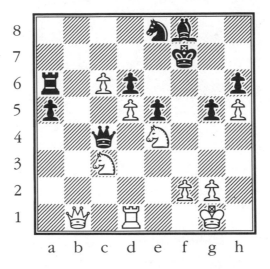

Black's forces are in no position to defend, so Jordy invests a knight to create a spectacular finish. **34.Nxg5+!! hxg5; 35.Qg6+ Ke7; 36.Qe6+.** Black resigned, since it is mate next move at d8.

*J*ordy won $20,000 toward college for winning the Valley Scholar award, given to 15 youths selected as the most outstanding students in Silicon Valley.

ASUKA & HIKARU Nakamura

12 AND 10 YEARS OLD

Asuka's was born Feb. 4, 1986, Hikaru Dec 9, 1987; in Osaka prefecture, Japan.

Hikaru deep in thought

Asuka and brother Hikaru Nakamura are the stepsons of famous trainer Sunil Weeramantry. A combination of Japanese, American and Sri Lankan backgrounds would seem ideal for chessplayers planning to perform on the international stage!

It wasn't Sunil that brought the brothers into the chess world. Their mother, Carolyn, was responsible for their early chess careers, long before she met her husband.

The link between chess and music is very strong. Gabe Kahane is the son of a prominent pianist and conductor, and I was also raised in a musical household and spent some time pursuing a career as a symphonic conductor. Another famous prodigy, Nigel Short, was a member of a rock band and many famous musicians have been chess enthusiasts. One thing that seems to frustrate such musician parents is the tendency for their kids to wind up preferring chess to music!

Asuka Nakamura won the 1992 National Kindergarten School Championship and was quickly recognized as a prodigy. He has won a total of eight national championships and holds a unique record in the Grade School Nationals where in five years of competition he has compiled the unbelievable record of 30 wins, not giving up a single draw or loss. He reached the expert class in 1996. He had a nice ride atop the chess prodigy world, but all records fall sooner or later. The day inevitably arrives when someone younger and more talented grabs the spotlight. Asuka knew this day would come, but was certainly surprised when the usurper turned out to be none other than his little brother, Hikaru!

> *A*suka won eight national championships and compiled the unbelievable record of 30 straight wins in the Grade School Nationals, not drawing or losing in five years!

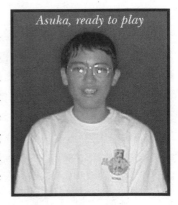
Asuka, ready to play

This didn't force Asuka to give up his chessboard, however. Asuka was the 1998 US Representative in the Pan American Boys Under-12 Championship and 1996 World Boys Under-10 Championship. He was awarded the 1997 Aspis Prize, a substantial chess scholarship that is awarded annually to the highest rated player under the age of 13 during that calendar year. When not playing chess, Asuka's life is filled with computers, violin and trombone, and a voracious appetite for basketball. He presently attends White Plains Middle School.

In 1998, Hikaru, just ten years old, set a new record by achieving the title of National Master when his rating topped the 2200 mark in April, as a result of a tournament in February. The record had previously been held by Vinay and Jordy. Hikaru's achievement earned him national television and newspaper fame.

Hikaru started playing at the age of seven, and made master in under three years! His first venture into competitive chess was at the 1995 U.S. Jr. Congress East where he won only one game. Then, in May that year, Asuka's team from Ridgeway school needed a fourth player. It was Hikaru to the rescue, but his contribution of two points in seven games was hardly an omen of future stardom.

Four influences fed his hunger for the game. His stepfather and brother played a major role, of course, but Hikaru also found a computer sparring partner sufficiently annoying that he felt a need to defeat the machine. That summer, his brother and step-father competed in the U.S. Open in Concord. Hikaru was informed that he was not ready to compete in that event. His answer was to set up residence in the skittles room and throw his 700+ rating at anyone who cared to challenge him. His favorite opponent was FM Oscar Tan who would hang his queen on purpose and pretend he had blundered. And, Hikaru believed him!

Hikaru's rapid ascent up the chess ladder began in October 1995 and is truly phenomenal. In two short years, he reached the 1800 level but seemed to have hit a plateau. Then, on New Year's Eve in 1997, when most kids are at a party or in bed, Hikaru upset International Master Jay Bonin, another

> *In 1998, Hikaru, just ten years old, became the youngest National Master ever, a record previously held by Vinay and Jordy.*

youngest-ever record. This inspired him to even higher goals. When Hikaru is playing, you can see the intensity in his face. There is a fierceness in evidence on and off the chessboard. He works intensively on chess, studying all aspects of the game.

Hikaru is a fanatic baseball fan, and hopes that he can enjoy the sort of season his favorite New York Yankees have been having. He follows their exploits at home and on the road, and is as passionate about baseball as he is about chess. Baseball is also his refuge from the pressures of the chess world. His favorite pastime is broadcasting play by plays on simulated Yankee games to his imaginary audience. Fortunately, the World Series will be over before Hikaru starts his challenge for the World Under-12 Championship. Meanwhile, the records keep falling, as Hikaru is now the youngest to beat an IM and GM. His win over Arthur Bisguier, presented later, was achieved when he was just ten years and four months old, breaking Vinay's record.

As with the other pairs of siblings in this book, it remains to be seen how their internal rivalry will affect their attitude toward the game. Asuka remains the more relaxed of the two, but he is used to looking over his shoulder, and now in front of him, where his fierce younger brother is an inevitable presence.

TWO OF OUR BEST GAMES

Asuka didn't earn a medal at this year's Pan American Championships but he did play some excellent chess, including this positional crush. The game starts out quietly. Asuka follows the sage advice of Wilhelm Steinitz, the first World Champion, in slowly accumulating advantages. His opponent makes no terrible blunders, but is slowly crushed to death.

ASUKA VS. DIEGO PRETTA
Pan American Boys Under 12 Championship, Brazil, 1998

1.e4 e5; 2.Nf3 Nf6; 3.Nc3 Nc6; 4.d4 exd4; 5.Nxd4 Bb4; 6.Nxc6 bxc6; 7.Bd3 d5; 8.exd5 cxd5; 9.0-0 0-0; 10.Bg5 Bxc3; 11.bxc3 h6; 12.Bh4 Qd6.

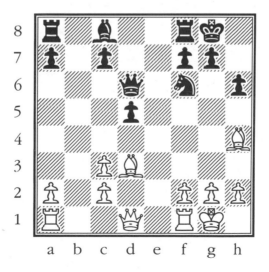

Asuka has played without much ambition so far, but has obtained the bishop pair, at the cost of weakening his queenside pawns.

13.Qf3 Bg4; 14.Qg3 Qxg3; 15.Bxg3 c6. The first part of the endgame sees Asuka slowly increase his positional advantage. **16.f3 Bd7; 17.Ba6 Bc8; 18.Bd3 Be6; 19.Rab1 Rfd8; 20.Rb7!** The occupation of the seventh rank is a significant achievement. **20...Rd7; 21.Rfb1 Kf8; 22.Rxd7 Bxd7; 23.Bd6+ Ke8; 24.Ba6.**

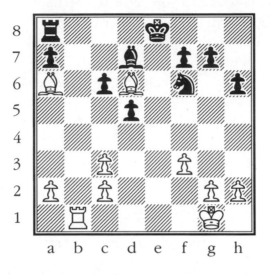

Black is getting squeezed, and the rook at a8 is running out of room. Therefore he offers an exchange of bishops. **24...Bc8; 25.Bxc8 Rxc8; 26.Rb7 Rd8; 27.Bc5.** The a-pawn is doomed. **27...Rd7; 28.Rxa7 Rxa7; 29.Bxa7.**

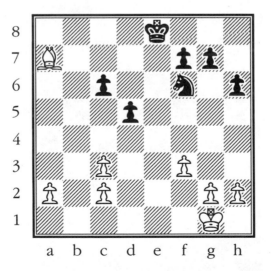

The endgame is winning for White, and Asuka presses home the point efficiently. **29...Ke7; 30.Kf2 Kd7; 31.Bd4 Ne8; 32.Ke2 c5; 33.Be3 Nc7; 34.Bf4 Kc6; 35.Bxc7 Kxc7; 36.Kd3 Kd6; 37.c4. Black resigned.** The king and pawn endgame is hopeless.

Hikaru is not afraid to face his rivals. Justin Sarkar is another promising junior player, and the two met in professional competition in the annual international tournament in Chicago.

HIKARU VS. JUSTIN SARKAR
Chicago International, 1998

1.e4 c5; 2.Nc3 e6; 3.Nf3 Nc6; 4.d4 cxd4; 5.Nxd4 d6; 6.Be3 Nf6; 7.Be2 Be7; 8.Qd2 0–0; 9.0–0–0.

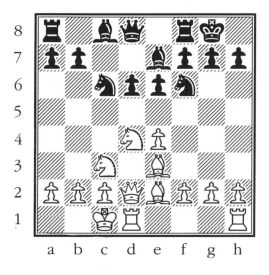

This is a very sharp variation of the Classical Sicilian. Castling on opposite wings usually leads to an exciting game. I am planning to attack on the kingside, and am prepared to deal with any threats Black can create on the opposite wing.

9...a6; 10.f4 Qc7; 11.g4 b5; 12.g5 Nd7; 13.f5 b4; 14.Nb1 Nc5; 15.Nxc6 Qxc6; 16.f6! This cracks open Black's defensive shell.

16...gxf6; 17.gxf6 Bxf6; 18.Rhg1+ Kh8; 19.Bh6 b3.

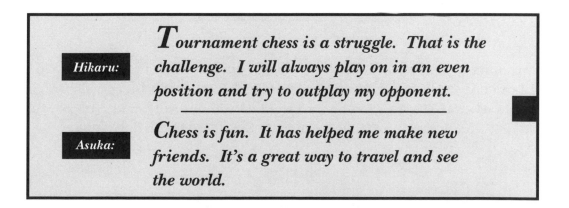

Hikaru: *Tournament chess is a struggle. That is the challenge. I will always play on in an even position and try to outplay my opponent.*

Asuka: *Chess is fun. It has helped me make new friends. It's a great way to travel and see the world.*

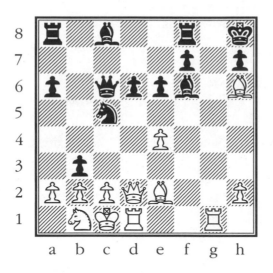

The attack is going well, but I have to be careful. **20.Bc4!;** 20.Qf4 would have let my opponent play 20...Bxb2+!; 21.Kxb2 Na4+; 22.Ka3 Qc5+; 23.Kxa4 Bd7+; 24.Bb5 (24.Kxb3 Rab8+ also leads to mate.) 24...axb5+; 25.Kxb3 Qc4+; 26.Kb2 Rxa2+; 27.Kc1 Rxc2#. **20...bxc2; 21.Qf4 cxd1Q+.** Who needs the rook, anyway?

22.Kxd1 Bd4.

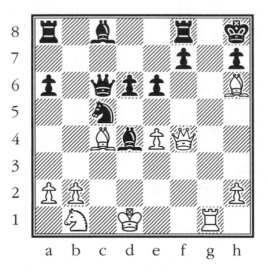

My other rook is attacked, but Black's king is defended only by the bishop at d4, and I can take care of that!; **23.e5! f5.** The only defense, but it isn't good enough. **24.Qxd4 d5; 25.Bxf8.** This bishop isn't finished with his work, and I am not finished on the dark squares! **25...dxc4; 26.Bg7+ Kg8; 27.Qd8+ Kf7; 28.Qf8#.**

JENNIFER & GREG *Shahade*

17 AND 19 YEARS OLD

Jennifer born Dec. 31, 1980, Greg born Dec. 22, 1978; in Philadelphia

Jennifer was selected as USCF "Player of the Month" in 1998!

The Shahade siblings got an early start in chess. They entered the Castle Chess Camp at an early age. Peter Kurzdorfer and I were two of Jenn's teachers when she was just six years old! Their father, Mike Shahade, is an accomplished FIDE Master.

Greg is also a rising star in chess, but at the grand old age of 19 he'll have to let his younger sister take the spotlight here.

Having an older brother who is better than you are is not much fun, and often the younger kids give up. Jordy's sister Marijo lost interest for a while, but is once again an enthusiastic player. In Jenn's case, she used her brother's phenomenal success as motivation. Her style is very aggressive, and she does not fear entering into the fiercest battles. Jenn even dares to adopt the dangerous Sicilian Dragon opening, with its ferocious middlegame. She is willing to put in the hard hours of study required by such daring strategies.

All that doesn't keep Jenn from enjoying herself. Her outgoing personality usually finds her in the middle of a large crowd at tournaments. Away from the chess scene she likes to join her competitors in whatever activity is present. If it involves competition, she thrives on challenging and defeating her male counterparts.

Jenn has had several great successes. She was selected as the Player of the Month for 1998. She is expected to receive the title of

First place in the 1993 National Junior High Championship brought Greg national recognition.

Woman International Master soon, having made a qualifying norm at the Saitek US Masters in Hawaii. She won the US Junior Open this year, following in her brothers impressive footsteps.

Greg has had considerable success himself. First place in the 1993 National Junior High School Championship brought him national recognition. In 1996, he tied for first in the National High School Championship and won the US Junior Open outright. He was a member of the 1996 Pan American Intercollegiate Championship team, the University of Maryland Baltimore County. Greg Shahade is a FIDE Master who is currently pursuing the International Master title.

TWO OF OUR BEST GAMES

JENNIFER VS. MAZZARELLI
US Open, Concord, 1995

1.e4 c5; 2.c3 Nf6; 3.e5 Nd5; 4.d4 cxd4; 5.Nf3 Nc6; 6.cxd4 e6; 7.Bd3.

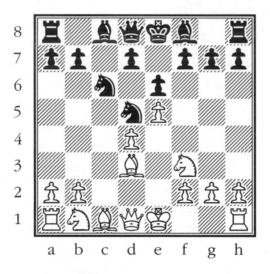

The normally quiescent Alapin Sicilian turns sharp here as Jenn adopts a very rare plan which is not even mentioned in the authoritative texts.

7...d6; 8.a3 Nde7; 9.Nc3 Ng6. Black wants to win the e-pawn and expects that White will capture at d6, leaving the pawn at d4 exposed. Jenn has more ambitious plans! **10.Qe2!?** At first glance, this seems to protect the pawn at e5. The queen has other duties, however, including the obligation to defend the bishop at d3.

10...dxe5; 11.dxe5 Ncxe5.

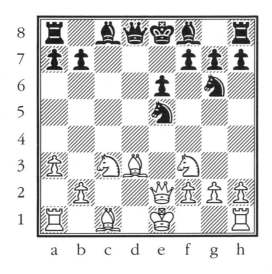

12.Bb5+! The check saves the bishop. 12.Nxe5 Nxe5; 13.Qxe5 Qxd3 would have been terrible for White.

12...Nd7. Forced, as otherwise Black loses a piece at e5. **13.h4** The kingside attack begins. Jenn has four pieces developed and will be able to castle quickly to either side of the board. Black does not have time to spare.

13...a6; 14.Ba4 Be7; 15.h5 Nh4; 16.Nxh4 Bxh4; 17.Qe4. The queen is safe on this central square, as the Black knight is pinned and cannot attack her. **17...Be7.** The bishop might have been more useful at f6, where it guards g7.

18.Bf4! 0–0; 19.0–0–0.

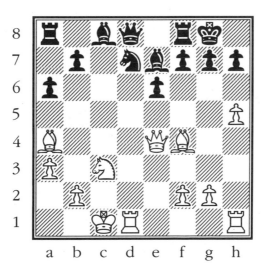

The pin on the d-file, advanced development, and potential kingside attack is well worth a pawn. Black sees a way to reduce the pressure by swapping bishops and breaking the pin. Perhaps there was no more useful plan, but the weakness of e7

was underestimated.

19...Bg5; 20.Bxg5 Qxg5+; 21.f4 Qe7. What choice was there. The knight needed defense and Black did not want to walk back into the pin. 21...Qd8; 22.Bxd7 Bxd7; 23.Qxb7 would have won a piece.

22.Nd5! The pin is now on the e-file, and the knight leaps into the fray. **22...Qc5+; 23.Bc2.** Black still has no time to catch a breath, the threat is mate at h7! **23...g6; 24.hxg6 hxg6; 25.f5!**

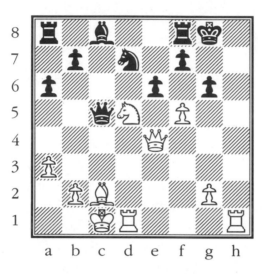

A wonderful finish. The White queen will get to h4.

25...exd5; 26.Qh4 Qe3+; 27.Kb1 forces the king to flee with **27...Kg7** but **28.Rd3!** brings a swift end to the game. The queen must abandon the c1–h6 diagonal, and then White mates quickly.

28...Qe2; 29.f6+ Nxf6; 30.Qh6+. Black resigned.

GREG'S TURN

Let's give Greg his due now. Here he crushes a young Candidate Master in a miniature. Shahade's quiet opening play is the prelude to a brutal attack which brings his opponent to his knees in just sixteen moves.

GREG VS. ANDY REEDER
Cardoza US Open, Kona, Hawaii, 1998

1.c4 e6; 2.Nc3 d5; 3.d4 c6; 4.Bf4 Nf6; 5.e3 Bd6; 6.Bg3 0-0; 7.Nf3 Bxg3; 8.hxg3 Nbd7; 9.Qc2 h6; 10.0-0-0 Qe7; 11.Rh4 dxc4; 12.Bxc4 e5; 13.Rdh1 exd4.

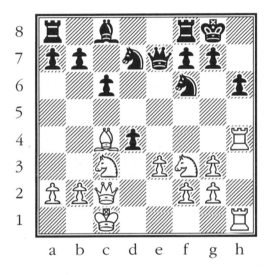

Black's formulaic opening strategy has failed to take into account White's aggressive intentions. With a fine rook sacrifice Greg forces mate in five moves.

14.Rxh6!! gxh6. 14...Qxe3+ would have delayed the end by one more move. **15.Qg6+.**

Black resigned because of 15...Kh8; 16.Rxh6+ Nh7; 17.Rxh7#.

OUR BIG TRIUMPHS!

Each of our young stars has already stunned the chess world by defeating much higher ranked opposition. This chapter contains games which helped to bring the young stars worldwide attention or added to an already illustrious profile. It is not easy to bring down a Grandmaster, especially under tournament conditions. The professional player has a wealth of experience, and knows better than to take a young opponent lightly.

On the contrary, young players are assumed to be under-rated. The ranking system takes time to catch up with current results, and improving players tend to hover below their actual playing strength. Indeed, young players are not welcome opponents for Grandmasters. There are fewer games floating around in databases, and young players often change openings until they find a good fit between their skills and particular opening strategies.

When a young player faces a Grandmaster, the goal is to keep the game in familiar territory. Winning moves are usually seen in the opening or middlegame. In the endgame, the vast experience of the Grandmaster is usually too much to overcome. There isn't much psychology at work. The Grandmaster set as many problems as possible for the less experienced opponent. The more balanced the position, the more pressure there is on the Grandmaster to take the initiative. It is when the professional is trying to find ways to improve winning chances that mistakes can be made. In the majority of games, the patience of the professional wins in the end, but often the prospect of a mere draw can lead to unwise decisions.

The games in this chapter show our young stars exploiting the changes that appear during a game. In a number of games, the prodigies take out veteran Grandmasters! Although chessplayers often peak in their 30s, experience has propelled many seniors into World Champion competition. Former World Champion Smyslov got to the Candidates' Final in 1984, in his 60s, and Viktor Korchnoi is enjoying tremendous sporting events this year. These Grandmasters do not make a single, horrible blunder but rather overlook a resource or two that their challenger managed to spot.

Publisher Avery Cardoza with the 1998 Cardoza US Open co-winners, Judit Polgar and Boris Gulko (left).

JENNIE

We start off with Jennie's recent win over veteran Grandmaster Arnold Denker, a former US Champion and still an active player in his 80s. Usually a Grandmaster can defeat a young player by relying on experience. Often the games head to complicated endings where younger players tend to be weak.

Watch what happens here.

JENNIE VS. GRANDMASTER ARNOLD DENKER
Cardoza US Open, Kona, Hawaii, 1998

1.e4 c5; 2.Nc3 d6; 3.g3 Nc6; 4.Bg2 Nf6; 5.d3 g6; 6.f4 Bg7; 7.Nf3 Bd7; 8.0–0 a6; 9.h3 Qc7; 10.Be3 0–0; 11.g4 e6; 12.Qe1 Rac8; 13.Qh4 b5; 14.f5.

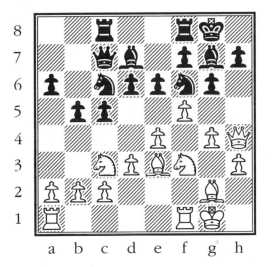

This bold pawn sacrifice lets the bishop at e3 join the attack on the kingside. **14...b4.** Black drives the knight back before taking the pawn. **15.Ne2 exf5; 16.Bh6!?** Another pawn is sacrificed, but more lines are opened. **16...fxg4; 17.Ng5 Nh5?** A natural reaction, closing some lines, but it is not enough.

There are two alternative defenses. One works, the other doesn't.

> *J*ennie chooses to launch an attack with a sacrifice that keeps all thoughts of an endgame far away from the board!

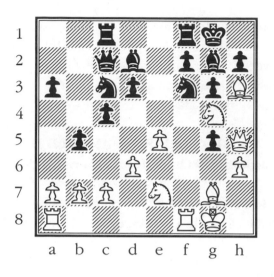

Capturing at h3 is too slow. 17...gxh3 would have been met by 18.Bxg7! hxg2 (18...Kxg7; 19.Rxf6 Kxf6; 20.Nf4 wins, as in the note to move 19.); 19.Rxf6 Kxg7 leads to mate in 5!; 20.Rxf7+ Rxf7; 21.Qxh7+ Kf6; 22.Qxf7+ Kxg5; 23.Qf4+ Kh5; 24.Ng3#

The proper defense is 17...Ne5; 18.Bxg7 Kxg7; 19.Rxf6 h6! (19...Kxf6; 20.Ne6+ Kxe6; 21.Nf4#); 20.Nxf7 Nxf7; 21.hxg4 g5; 22.Qf2 Bxg4 would have given Black a serious advantage.

After Denker's choice, blocking the h-file with the knight, the game continued **18.Bxg7 Kxg7; 19.hxg4.**

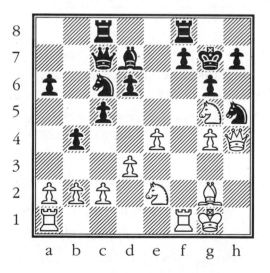

19...f6. The knight cannot retreat to f6, because Jennie would have ripped open the position with a powerful exchange sacrifice. 19...Nf6; 20.Rxf6! Kxf6; 21.Nf4!!

The discovered check is held back, and the other knight leaps into the game, threatening Nd5+, forking the king and queen.

20.Nh3 Bxg4. The knight at h5 was trapped. **21.Qxg4 Ne5; 22.Qe6 Rce8; 23.Qb3.** Black does not have sufficient compensation for the missing bishop. **23...g5; 24.d4!** Open lines are needed to put the extra piece to use.

24...cxd4; 25.Nxd4 Qc5; 26.Qe3. The threat is 27.Nxg5 hxg5; 28.Qxg5+ when the knight at h5 falls. **26...Nc4; 27.Nf5+! Qxf5.** 27...Kg6; 28.Qxc5 dxc5; 29.b3 Nd2; 30.Rfe1 Re5; 31.Rad1 Rd8; 32.Re3! White plans Rd3, when the knight at d2 is doomed. 32...g4; 33.Nf2 and White will win.

28.Qa7+ Rf7; 29.Qxf7+ Kxf7; 30.exf5.

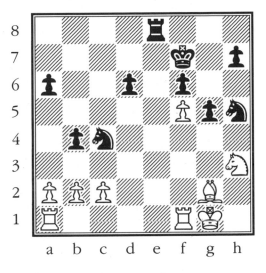

Black's two pawns do not come close to the power of White's extra bishop, and the Black pawns on the queenside are weak.

30...Ne3; 31.Rfe1 Ng3. 31...Nxc2; 32.Bd5+ Kf8; 33.Rxe8+ Kxe8; 34.Rc1 Nd4; 35.Rc4 Nxf5; 36.Rxb4 Black has only three pawns for the rook, and none of them are threatening to advance very far. **32.a3 bxa3.** 32...Nxc2; 33.Bd5+ Kf8; 34.Rxe8+ Kxe8; 35.Rb1 bxa3; 36.bxa3 Nxf5; 37.Rb8+ Kd7; 38.Rb7+ Kd8; 39.Rxh7 Nfe3; 40.Be6 d5; 41.Rf7 Nxa3; 42.Rxf6 Ke7; 43.Rg6 and the remaining pawns fall quickly.

33.Rxa3 Ngxf5; 34.Rxa6 d5; 35.Ra7+ Ke6; 36.Nf2 h5; 37.Nd1 d4.

The advancing kingside pawns are menacing, but not worth a rook. In any case, Black's pieces remain so tied down that a little move brings home the point quickly.

38.c3! Ke5; 39.cxd4+ Kf4; 40.Nxe3 Nxe3; 41.Ra3! A double pin! The knight cannot move because the rook on e8 falls, or mate.**41...g4.** Not 41...Ng4??; 42.Rf3#. **42.Raxe3 Rxe3; 43.Rxe3 Kxe3; 44.d5.** Black resigned.

IRINA

Irina has many chances to face experienced Grandmasters in professional competition. This year she has enjoyed sufficient sponsorship to be able to play matches against top competition. This game shows her beating a Grandmaster!

IRINA VS. GRANDMASTER ARTHUR BISGUIER
3rd Match Game, Parsippany 1998

1.d4 d5; 2.c4 e6; 3.Nc3 Nf6; 4.cxd5 exd5; 5.Bg5 Nbd7; 6.e3 Bb4.

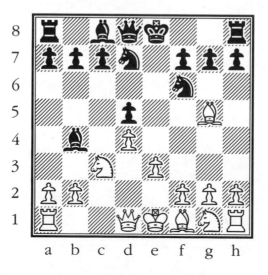

This opening is known as the Manhattan Variation. It is very sharp, leading to complications early in the game. The veteran Grandmaster perhaps counted on Irina not being familiar with the theory, but she plays the approved moves..

7.Bd3 c5; 8.Nge2 h6. 8...c4; 9.Bc2 is known to be good for White, and in fact recently Black has gotten clobbered using that approach. **9.Bh4 cxd4; 10.exd4.** The exchange of pawns leads to a sterile pawn structure, but White's pieces are in a better position to form attacking batteries. **10...0–0; 11.0–0 Nb6; 12.Bc2 Re8; 13.Qd3.**

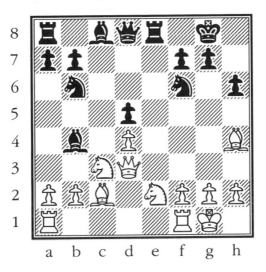

Irina is building up a formidable attack on the kingside. The Black king is defended just by a knight, which can easily be removed. The Grandmaster finds a way to "punt." Realizing that the game is going badly, Bisguier decides to give up the pawn at d5, hoping that White's own d-pawn will prove weak enough to snare later on in the game. Already Bisguier is no longer thinking of winning, but just surviving. **13...g6; 14.Bb3 Bf8; 15.Bxf6 Qxf6; 16.Nxd5 Nxd5; 17.Bxd5 Be6; 18.Bxe6 Qxe6.**

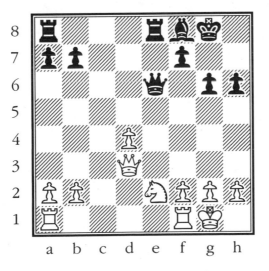

This position is almost an endgame, with White enjoying a clear pawn advantage. Black has no real counterplay, but the d-pawn cannot advance far without becoming further weakened. Irina properly concentrates on getting her pieces into useful positions.

19.Nc3 Rad8; 20.Rfd1 Bc5. This takes advantage of the pin on the queen by the rook at d8. The pawn shrugs and moves forward. **21.d5 Qe5; 22.Rac1 Bb4; 23.g3!** Irina want to play the rook from c1 to e2, via c2, but can't do so immediately. Her king could easily get trapped on the back rank, for example 23.Rc2 Bxc3; 24.Rxc3 Rxd5 picks off the pawn, because 25.Qxd5 loses to 25...Qe1+!; 26.Rxe1 Rxe1#. **23...a6; 24.Rc2 Bxc3; 25.bxc3 Rd6; 26.c4!**

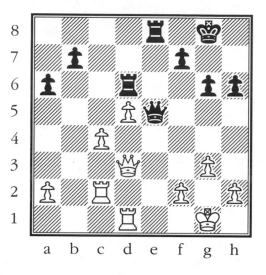

The game is effectively over. Black has no time to advance the pawn to b5, and the pawns march forward, assisted by the heavy artillery. Irina executes perfectly. **26...Red8; 27.Re2 Qh5; 28.Rde1 Qg5; 29.Re5 Qf6; 30.c5 R6d7; 31.Qe4.** Tripling pieces on the e-file allows Irina to infiltrate.

31...Kg7; 32.Re3 Rc8; 33.d6 b6; 34.Re7 Rxe7; 35.dxe7 Re8; 36.Qb7.

In this game, Irina takes veteran Grandmaster Arthur Bisguier to school in the endgame, usually the strongest part of his game.

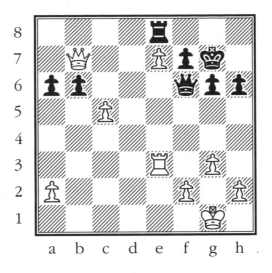

The Grandmaster resigned, as there is no way to stop 37.Qd7, forcing the rook off the promotion square.

HIKARU

Hikaru's opponent in this game, International Master Alexander Stripunsky, has already earned his qualifications for the Grandmaster title and should receive it shortly. Nevertheless, he was unable to defeat Nakamura in this game.

INTERNATIONAL MASTER STRIPUNSKY VS. HIKARU
Marshall Chess Club Tournament, New York, 1998

1.e4 c5; 2.Nf3 e6; 3.c3 d5; 4.exd5 exd5; 5.d4 Nc6; 6.Be3 cxd4; 7.Nxd4 Nf6; 8.Be2 Be7; 9.0–0 0–0; 10.Nd2.

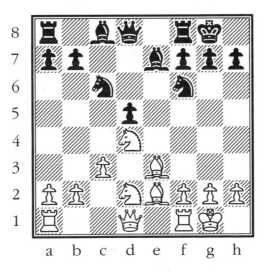

I don't know whether Hikaru was familiar with the previous tries in this position, which were played long before he was born!

10...Be6; 11.N2b3 Qd7; 12.Re1 Rfd8. Black protects the isolated pawn with three pieces. White cannot increase the pressure, so he captures the bishop at e6. **13.Nxe6 fxe6; 14.Bg5 e5; 15.Bf1 h6; 16.Bh4 a6; 17.Qc2 Rac8; 18.Rad1 b5.** Black's position has a few holes.

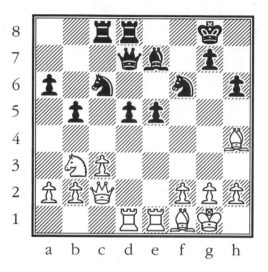

White clearly has the better game, since Black is reduced to passive defense. **19.Qg6 Qe6; 20.Rd3 Qf7.** The kingside attack is repulsed, but at the cost of going into an endgame where Black's pawns are weak.

21.Qf5 Ne8; 22.Qxf7+ Kxf7; 23.Bxe7 Kxe7.

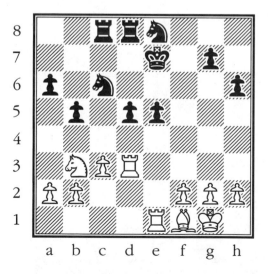

Black's position is a little suspect. There are three groups of pawns, known as pawn islands, compared to two for White. In general, the fewer islands, the better.

The pawns are under attack from rooks on open files, and White can infiltrate with Nc5. All in all, a tough defense awaits Black. **24.Nc5 Ra8; 25.h4 Nf6; 26.f3 g5; 27.hxg5 hxg5; 28.Rde3 Re8; 29.b4 Kd6; 30.Rd1 a5!?**

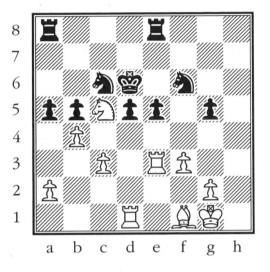

The best practical chance. Black's position is under pressure and only by opening up lines can Hikaru get into the game. Understanding that his rooks are inactive, he gives up the pawn at b5 to open up the a-file.

31.Bxb5 axb4; 32.cxb4 Rxa2! The point. Not 32...Nxb4; 33.Nb7+ Kc7; 34.Bxe8 Rxe8; 35.Rc3+ Kxb7; 36.Rb1 and Black is the exchange down. **33.Rc3?** Wrong move order! 33.Nb7+! would have won material. 33...Kc7; 34.Rc3 Re6; 35.Na5 piles on the pin, and Black would have been forced to play 35...Rxa5; 36.bxa5 d4; 37.Rxc6+ Rxc6; 38.Bxc6 Kxc6; 39.Rb1. Black would go down to defeat.

33...Nd4. Because White played Rc3 before Nf7, Black has time to react and climb back into the game. **34.Nb7+ Ke6.**

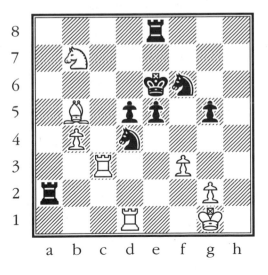

> *H*ikaru's bold play reaps its rewards. The rook on e8 is hanging, but if the bishop takes it, then the Black knight jumps to e2, forking the king and rook, and creating additional threats. White can't easily avoid losing material.

35.Rxd4. 35.Bxe8 Ne2+; 36.Kh2 Nxc3; 37.Rc1 Nxe8; 38.Rxc3 d4 is a horrid endgame for White. 35.Nc5+ Kf5; 36.Bxe8 Ne2+; 37.Kh2 Nxc3; 38.Rd3 Nxe8; 39.Rxc3 d4 is not much of an improvement. **35...exd4; 36.Rc6+ Ke5.** Black's king is in the middle of the board but it is in no danger. **37.Nc5!?** 37.Rxf6 Kxf6; 38.Bxe8 wins material but the d-pawn flies. 38...d3; 39.Bb5 d2; 40.Be2 allows Black to win the bishop by promoting the pawn and pinning along the first rank, but picking off the b-pawn first is even stronger. 40...Rb2; 41.Nc5 Rxb4; 42.Kf2 Rb1; 43.Ke3 d1Q; 44.Bxd1 Rxd1; 45.Nd3 Ke6 should win for Black in the long run..

37...Re7. White is in serious trouble. **38.Nd3+.** 38.g4!? would have allowed Black to infiltrate. 38...Kf4!! 39.Rxf6+ Kg3 and the White king is doomed. 40.Re6 Ra1+; 41.Bf1 Rh7 with mate in four, the immediate threat being ...Rh1+ and ...Rxf1#.

38...Kf5; 39.Nc1 This is a very awkward defense. It allows Hikaru to make the most of the rooks. **39...Re1+! 40.Kh2 Ra1; 41.Ne2 Rh1+; 42.Kg3 Nh5+. White resigned**, because of 43.Kf2 Raf1#.

VINAY

In the 6th round of the 1996 American Open, Vinay, already a National Master, had his chance to take on the same veteran Grandmaster. Both were doing well in the competition, and faced each other on the sixth board.

Vinay's win brought him to the top of the field.

GRANDMASTER ARTHUR BISGUIER VS. VINAY
American Open, Los Angeles, 1996

1.d4 d5 2.c4 e6; 3.Nc3 c6; 4.e3 Bd6; 5.Nf3 f5.

The Stonewall Dutch formation is very solid, but also lets Black play for an attack on the kingside.

6.Ne5 Nf6; 7.f4 0–0; 8.b3 Ne4; 9.Nxe4 fxe4; 10.Be2 b6; 11.0–0 Bb7; 12.Bg4 Qe7; 13.Bb2 Nd7; 14.Rc1.

> *T*here were hundreds of players in the competition, and Vinay's win over the Grandmaster did not go unnoticed!

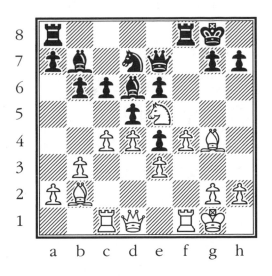

White's pieces are more actively placed compared to mine.

14...Nf6; 15.Bh3 c5; 16.g4 Rad8; 17.g5 Ne8; 18.Qg4 Nc7; 19.Qh5?! This throws away White's advantage and initiative. 19.g6 is much better, keeping the attack going. If then 19...Bxe5 (19...Rf6; 20.Qh5 hxg6; 21.Nxg6 Qe8; 22.f5 gives White a powerful attack. White's actual move is too slow, and gives me time to rid myself of the knight on e5 and drive away White's queen.); 20.gxh7+ Kxh7; 21.Qh5+ Kg8; 22.fxe5 is good for White.

19...Bxe5; 20.fxe5 g6! This is a good move, putting the question to the enemy queen.

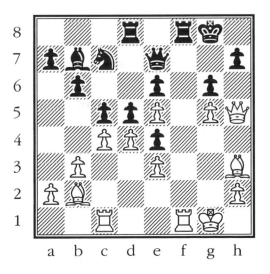

21.Qh6? The queen is too isolated here, away from where the action will be. 21.Qh4 keeps watch over the g-pawn and can also retreat to guard the king. In reply I had planned 21...Rf3 which I think gives me a good game.

21...Rf3!; 22.Rxf3. Since the e-pawn is hanging, White is almost forced to exchange on f3 now. After 22.Rce1 , 22...Rdf8 is good for Black. **22...exf3; 23.Rf1 Rf8; 24.Ba3?** A very bad move which costs White the game. **24...dxc4; 25.bxc4 f2+!**

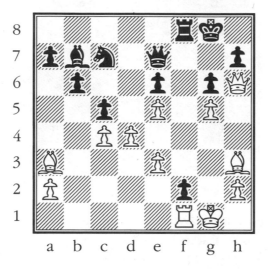

This wins by force. White's queen doesn't cover f2 and can't get back in time to help out on defense. **26.Rxf2 Rxf2; 27.Kxf2 Qf7+; 28.Ke1.** Other moves don't save White either. **28...Qf3; 29.Bc1 Qh1+; 30.Kd2 Bf3; 31.Kc2 Qd1+; 32.Kb2 Be4**. White resigned, having no way to avert checkmate.

JORDY

This game was played in a competition where each player had just five minutes to complete all moves. It came in the midst of an extraordinary summer which got Jordy off to a bad start at the US Cadet but then saw him earn honors at major US events. He had just completed a fine performance at the Saitek US Masters, defeating Grandmaster Leonid Shamkovich along the way, when he decided to warm up for the Cardoza US Open by playing in a blitz tournament.

It brought him 10 minutes of fame!

Jordy has managed quite a few significant upsets, but beating the greatest female player of all time was certainly one of his greatest thrills. Judit Polgar is among the top 20 players in the world and was on the eve of a great success at the Cardoza US Open.

JORDY VS. GRANDMASTER JUDIT POLGAR
Three Island Blitz Tour, Honolulu, HI, 1998

1.d4 Nf6; 2.c4 g6; 3.Nc3 Bg7; 4.e4 d6; 5.Be2 0–0; 6.Bg5 Na6. The development of the knight at a6 has been a trend in many of the variations of the King's Indian Defense. **7.Qd2 c5.** 7...e5; 8.d5 c6 is a popular alternative.

8.d5 e6; 9.Nf3 exd5; 10.exd5.

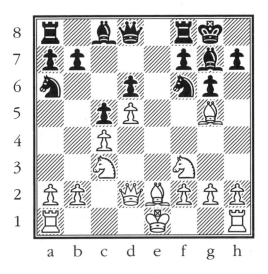

Polgar is combining two different systems. The plan with ...c5 and the exchange of central pawns is a traditional one. The knight does not usually travel to a6 in that line. **10...Nc7; 11.0–0 Bd7.** Black aims for ...b5, but it is not easily achieved. **12.Bf4 Qe7; 13.Rfe1 Rfe8; 14.Bf1 Qf8; 15.h3 Nh5.**

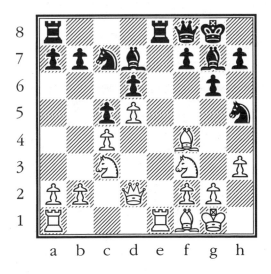

16.Bh2 Bh6. A good move which brings Black rough equality. Inevitably, rooks will be exchanged on the e-file. **17.Qc2 Nf6; 18.Bd3 Rxe1+; 19.Rxe1 Re8; 20.Rxe8 Bxe8; 21.a3 b5?!** Too ambitious, even for a blitz game.

22.cxb5 Nfxd5; 23.Nxd5 Nxd5; 24.Be4! Nc7; 25.Qd3. Jordy is willing to exchange the double pawn at b5 for the enemy pawn at d6. **25...d5.** 25...Bxb5; 26.Qxd6 Qxd6; 27.Bxd6 Ne6 would have been a bit better for White, because Black's queenside pawns are weak. **26.Bxc7 dxe4; 27.Qxe4 Bxb5.**

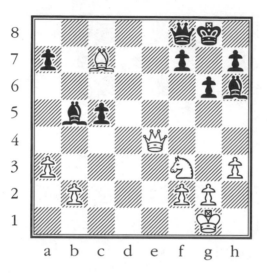

Black still has weak pawns, but has a potentially strong pair of bishops. White must play accurately to preserve the advantage.

28.Qd5! Be2. 28...Bc1; 29.Bd6 Qc8; 30.Be5 forces Black to worry about the kingside. **29.Ne5!** Polgar cannot cope with the pressure at c5 and f7. **29...Bg7; 30.Bd6 Qe8; 31.Qxc5 h5; 32.Qd5 a6?** Overlooking a simple threat. **33.Nxg6 Qb5; 34.Ne7+! Kh7; 35.Qxf7 Qg5; 36.Bf4** and Polgar resigned.

Judit got her revenge against Jordy a few days later in the Cardoza US Open, in tournament competition. The rematch was not particularly pleasant for him!

Jordy faces superstar Judit Polgar in a blitz game

JENNIFER

Al Chow is an experienced FIDE master who was once a rising young star. Jennifer showed him no respect, and went right after his king.

JENNIFER – FIDE MASTER ALBERT CHOW
World Open, Philadelphia, 1998

This position was reached after nineteen moves. Jennifer's queen is attacked, but rather than retreat, she used a bold sacrifice to slash open the enemy position.

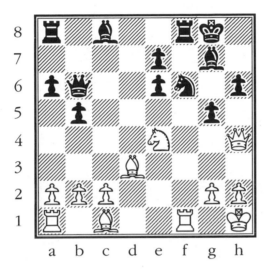

20.Bxg5!! hxg5; 21.Nxg5 Rd8; 22.Bh7+ Kf8; 23.Qh5. This move is possible because the rook at f1 pins the enemy knight to the king, so the queen cannot be captured. **23...Bd7; 24.Qf7#.**

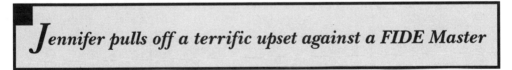

Jennifer pulls off a terrific upset against a FIDE Master

ASUKA

Asuka's biggest upset was against Senior Master Rick Bauer, a former Connecticut State Champion. Asuka adopts the Chigorin Variation of the Spanish Game, an opening which is over 100 years old!

Another powerful player is about to be taken down by one of our Whiz Kids

SENIOR MASTER RICK BAUER VS ASUKA
Newburgh, NY, 1998

1.e4 e5; 2.Nf3 Nc6; 3.Bb5 a6; 4.Ba4 Nf6; 5.0-0 Be7; 6.Re1 b5; 7.Bb3 d6; 8.c3 0-0; 9.h3 Na5; 10.Bc2 c5; 11.d4 Qc7; 12.Nbd2 Ne8.

You won't find this move in the books! Doesn't seem to risk immediate refutation however, and Black does manage to equalize. Black's plan is similar to a familiar one with Black retreating the knight to d7 and then placing the bishop at f6, putting more pressure on the center.

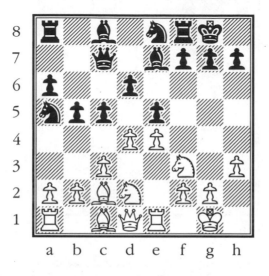

13.Nf1 Nc4; 14.b3 Nb6; 15.Bb2 Bf6; 16.Rc1. The rook does not seem to do much here, but the idea is that after Black exchanges at d4, the c-file can be opened. **16...g6; 17.Ne3 Bb7; 18.dxe5 dxe5; 19.Nd5 Bxd5; 20.exd5 Rd8; 21.Be4 Nd6.**

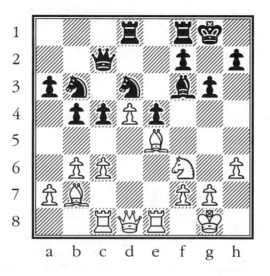

The knight which sat passively at e8 now finds useful employment. 22.Qe2?! Black controls c4, so this move accomplishes nothing. **22...c4; 23.Ba3 Rfe8; 24.Bxd6 Qxd6; 25.bxc4 Nxc4.** Black has the advantage, because White has weak pawns at a2, c3 and d5. **26.a4 Bg7; 27.axb5 axb5; 28.Rb1 f5!** This wins the d-pawn. **29.Bd3 Qxd5; 30.Bxc4 bxc4; 31.Rb4 e4; 32.Nd4 Rc8; 33.Rd1 Qc5; 34.Qb2.**

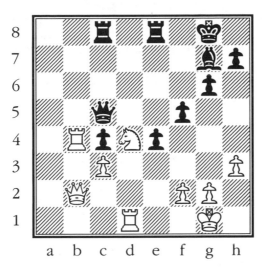

Converting the extra pawn into a full point on the crosstable is well within Asuka's ability! **34...e3!; 35.fxe3 Rxe3; 36.Rb5 Qe7; 37.Qb1 Rxc3** Black could have resigned here. The rest is trivial.

38.Nf3 Qe3+; 39.Kh1 Rb3; 40.Rxb3 cxb3; 41.Re1 Qc3; 42.Ng5 Bh6; 43.h4 Bxg5; 44.hxg5 b2; 45.Qa2 Kh8; 46.Qe6 Qxe1+. White resigned.

This chapter showed off the best triumphs of the Whiz Kids, but life is not always so rosy. Now we'll take a look at the other side of the coin, the terrible defeats where a might blunder or series of blunders not only change the course of the game, but sometimes, a tournament.

OUCH! OUR WORST LOSSES!

Everyone makes mistakes. There isn't a chess player alive who hasn't played an embarrassingly bad move. We'll take a look at instructive blunders by each of our young stars, but to put the matter in proper perspective, let's start with a whopper by no less than the reigning United States Champion, Joel Benjamin.

Joel was a prodigy himself. He was the chess consultant on IBM's Deep Blue project, and won the United States Championship in 1987 and 1997. He made a brief appearance in the film *Searching for Bobby Fischer*, which was the story of another chess prodigy, Josh Waitzkin.

A CHAMPION STUMBLES

BENJAMIN VS. GUFELD
Saitek US Masters, Honolulu, Hawaii 1998

White has an extra pawn, but is short of time and must move quickly. Failing to notice the threat, Benjamin moved his king to e5 with **80.Ke5??** Gufeld leaped for joy after he played **80...Qe6** with an epaulette mate.

Following is the final position.

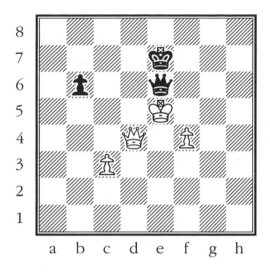

And Gets His Revenge...

A true champion doesn't let such blunders remain unavenged. In the very next tournament, a week later, Benjamin took revenge in a brutal yet elegant fashion.

BENJAMIN VS. GUFELD
Cardoza US Open, Kona, Hawaii, 1998

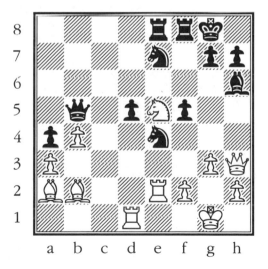

White doesn't seem to have any way to get at the enemy king, and his rook is under attack at e2. Benjamin finds a brilliant way to open up the game.

30.Rxe4!! fxe4. This is the only legal capture, since the d-pawn is pinned to the king by the bishop at a2.

31.Qe6+ Kh8; 32.Qxh6!!

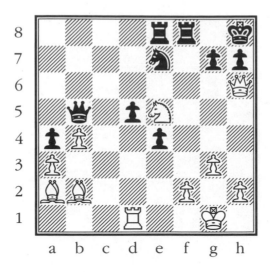

The queen is sacrificed, but capturing it would lead to checkmate after 32...gxh6; 33.Nf7+ (A discovered double check from the bishop at b2 and knight at f7!) 33...Kg8; 34.Nh6#. So Gufeld played **32...Nf5**, but the amazed crowd saw Benjamin leave the queen attacked by both pawn and knight, choosing the devastating **33.Ng6+ Kg8; 34.Rxd5!!** Black resigned.

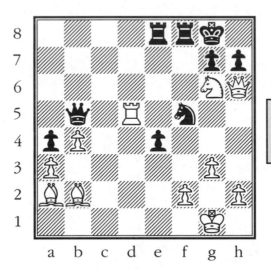

Joel Benjamin's "Mona Lisa."

If Black captured the queen, then White would take Black's queen with the rook, exposing a discovered check from the bishop at a2. Black would have to stick the rook in the way at f7, where it could be captured. White winds up with a decisive material advantage.

So even the best players blunder from time to time. Our young stars learned important lessons from their costly mistakes. We'll examine some of them now.

TWO WHIZ KIDS FALL SHORT

For Jordy and Vinay, the menacing rival was French prodigy Etienne Bacrot, who became the world's youngest Grandmaster in 1996. Home schooled, with full time training provided by a sponsor, it was hard for anyone to keep up with Etienne in the 1990s.

Jordy tells the tale of one of his most disappointing tournaments. Competitive chess tournaments offer plenty of opportunities for spectacular failure.

Jordy's Tells His Tale...

"When I was ten years old, I traveled as the U.S. representative to Slovakia to play in the World Youth Chess Championships for boys ten and under. I had started out the 11-round tournament with a bang, winning my first three games. In the third round, I defeated the French candidate Etienne Bacrot. Unbeknownst to me, he had won the European chess championship and later became the youngest Grandmaster in the world.

"After this stunning upset, everyone expected me to sweep the tournament and win the World Championship outright. I was walking on clouds. The next game brought me back down to earth. Playing with the black pieces, I faced Sekhar Ganguly of India. Perhaps because of my win over Bacrot, he offered me a draw very early on. I declined, proceeded to botch the game and lose miserably.

"The following round I had White against the Slovakian player, Federic Pavel. Again I fouled up a fine position and was extremely lucky to draw the game. In fact, Federic handed me the draw, having failed to see an easy win in the endgame. After this narrow escape, I played with the black pieces against Marcin Szymanski from Poland. I blundered for the third game in a row, and this time I wasn't as lucky. I lost.

"You can imagine how I felt. I had been leading the tournament, now I had only three and a half points out of a possible six. It was the worst moment in my chess career."

At age ten, America's youngest master felt like the world's youngest failure.

"I recall feeling an overwhelming determination to win, to overcome these losses. There were still five games left in the World Championship if I won every single one of them, I'd still have a chance for a medal.

"In the remaining rounds I faced other ten-year-olds from the Philippines, France, Ukraine, and Uzbekistan. I played solidly each day and won every game.

> *You can imagine how I felt. I had been leading the tournament, now I had only three and a half points out of a possible six. It was the worst moment in my chess career.*

"The last round was particularly interesting. My opponent was Kuliev Sarkan of Azerbaijan. Showing that chess is not just about bloodthirsty competition, one of the Russian candidates gave me a copy of his game with Kuliev to aid me in my preparation. Miraculously, I was now playing on the second board, adjacent to Etienne Bacrot on Board One. Kuliev played a tricky opening line in an effort to trap me, but his plan backfired and he ended up stumbling first in the precarious position. I beat him, finishing with eight and a half points out of eleven rounds.

"My score earned me the silver medal, behind gold medallist Etienne Bacrot, who had won every game after his loss to me. In this case, when faced with defeat, I somehow found the resources to bounce back and turn things around. I wish I could say the same about other occasions, when the outcome was less positive."

Vinay suffered a disaster against Bacrot, also in World Youth Championship competition. Vinay tells about his game...

BACROT VS. VINAY
World Youth Chess Championships, Sao Lorenzo, Brazil, 1995

1.d4. When this game was played, Ettiene was in first place with 5.5 out of 6, and I was in clear second with 5.0 out of 6. **1...d5; 2.c4 e6; 3.Nf3 c6.** This is the Semi-Slav Defense, which later became one of my favorites. Here I was using it for the first time. **4.g3 Bd6; 5.Bg2 Nf6; 6.0–0 0–0; 7.Qc2 Nbd7; 8.Nbd2 Qe7; 9.Re1.**

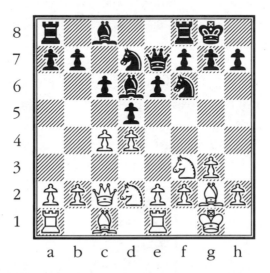

I had never played this opening before and it already begins to show. Black's setup with his Bishop on d6, Queen on e7, and Knight on d7, all point to the central break, e6-e5. 9...e5 would have been stronger.

With 10.cxd5 White would like to give Black an isolated queen pawn if possible.

10...Nxd5!? (10...cxd5 is of course possible. 11.dxe5 Nxe5; 12.Nxe5 Bxe5; 13.Nf3 Bd6; 14.b3. Even with an isolated queen pawn, Black has activity.) 11.e4 would have been logical. After 11...N5f6!?; 12.Nc4 Bb4 (Not 12...exd4? because 13.e5 and White wins.) 13.Re2 exd4; 14.e5 Nd5; 15.Bg5, White has an obviously better position.

Another idea was 11...Nb4; 12.Qb3 exd4; 13.Nxd4, where White threatens Nf5. I could have stopped this with 13...g6 but after 14.e5! Black has an unpleasant choice. 14...Bxe5?! is a poor move. 15.N2f3 Nd5; 16.Bf4 f6; 17.Nxe5 fxe5; 18.Bxd5+ cxd5; 19.Qxd5+ Kh8; 20.Nf3 White is winning. 14...Bc7 is better but Black still has the worse game. 15.N2f3 With threats like Bg5 and e6, White has a clear edge.

Instead, I chose **9...b6.** The game continued **10.e4 dxe4; 11.Ng5 e3?!** This voluntarily gives up the pawn. 11...Bb7; 12.Ndxe4 Bc7 would be similar to what happened except that White's rook is on e1 instead of e3.

12.Rxe3 Bb7; 13.Nde4 Bc7?! 13...Nxe4 is what I should have played. White cannot capture with the bishop because the knight at g5 hangs. On 14.Nxe4, I would have played 14...Bc7 and Black can push his c-pawn to c5 soon. 14.Rxe4 Nf6; 15.Re2 h6 might have been tried. White has a slight edge due to having more space, but this is only a minimal advantage.

14.Nc3 h6; 15.d5 cxd5? 15...hxg5 was forced. 16.dxc6 Bxc6; 17.Bxc6 Rac8. White has a slight edge, but Black can still put up a tough fight because of his development advantage. **16.Nxd5.**

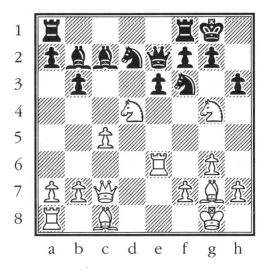

16...Nxd5?? The position was not good for Black, but this is just horrible. I hadn't even seen the checkmate mate until he played it. 16...Bxd5; 17.cxd5 hxg5; 18.dxe6 looks overpowering but Black has a saving move. 18...Ne5!; 19.exf7+ Qxf7; 20.Bxa8 Rxa8 is not so bad for Black.

17.Qh7# This was a huge loss to me, but I rebounded and finished tied for second place while Bacrot went on to win a clear gold medal.

THE GIRLS' NIGHTMARE

The Czech town of Bratislava played host to the 1993 World Youth Championships. Both Jennie and Irina were competing for championships. Each suffered a humiliating disaster, walking straight into a checkmate in a winning position! Jennie tells the tale of her most embarrassing moment.

"Last round of the World Girls Under 14 Championship, I am playing for a chance to be among the top 10. I am two bishops up, and get checkmated in one move by a pawn. What can be worse?"

RUTKOWSKA VS. JENNIE
World Girls Under-14 Championship, Bratislava, Czech Republic, 1993

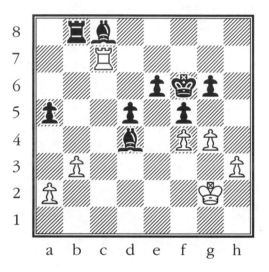

Jennie is up a rook and a bishop with an easy win. Capturing on g4 would have been simplest, but after **37...Ba6??** there was nothing left but tears after **38.g5#.**

Irina suffered an identical fate! With a huge advantage in an easily winning position she stumbled into mate in one. We don't have the record of the final position, but it was just as embarrassing and brought her to tears. She had allowed herself a bit of a premature celebration, but in chess, as in most sports, "it ain't over 'till it's over!"

This kind of disaster can be very painful, but as long as it is not repeated time will eventually heal the wounds. Even the best of players has fallen into such a mess at least once, and lived to tell the tale.

CHESS TOURNAMENTS

Do you like to travel? If the answer is yes, then you'll find that chess is the ticket to adventure all over the world. All of the 157 member nations of the World Chess Federation hold some form of tournaments, and most offer tournaments open to all players. Hundreds of major tournaments are held each year.

Let's consider a sample of the attractions offered in 1998/99, where our featured players have competed or are likely to compete.

July 1998: Saitek US Masters or Waikiki Open, Honolulu

August 1998: Cardoza US Open, Kona, Hawaii

September 1998: State Championships (usually Labor Day Weekend)

October 1998: World Youth Championships, Oropesa de Mar, Spain

November 1998: American Open, Los Angeles

December 1998: World Championships and related events, Las Vegas

January 1999: Suncoast Open, Australia

February 1999: US Amateur Teams (East, West, Midwest, South)

March 1999: New York Open, National Open, Las Vegas and Hawaii Chess Festival

April 1999: National High School/Jr. HS/ Elementary Championships

May 1999: First Saturday Internationals, Budapest, Hungary

June 1999: Politiken Cup, Copenhagen Denmark

July 1999: Universe Open, San Francisco or World Open, Philadelphia

Chess tournaments are held all over the country, and most of the games played by our young stars were in formal competitions. Tournaments range from modest weekend affairs with trophy prizes to the World Championship competition where the prize fund is $3,000,000! In many professional competitions, the participants have all their expenses paid and receive an "appearance fee" which can be tens of thousands of dollars.

The standard form of tournament is called a **Swiss System**. There is no elimination. Each round, players are paired with others who share the same score. After the first round, all the winners play another winner, losers are paired with losers, and those whose first game ended in a draw face each other. Weekend tournaments usually have 4-5 rounds. Major national events have 6-7 rounds, and international tournaments are 9-11 rounds. One nice thing about this system is that when you lose, you usual face weaker competition, and it is easy to work your way back into contention.

Some competitions are designed to pack as much chess as possible into a short period of time, while others have a leisurely pace, so that players can do some sightseeing and relax. Most American tournaments are of the first type, with a few exceptions, such as the Hawaii International Chess Festival. Europeans and the rest of the world tends to prefer the second type.

Often tournaments are held in resorts, for example along the Spanish coast of the Mediterranean, the Balearic Islands, the Canary Islands, Isle of Man, Cannes and Hungary's Lake Balaton. Chess tournaments are held in virtually every major city in the world. In America, the biggest tournaments are held in Las Vegas, Los Angeles, New York, and Philadelphia.

Entry fees range from about $10 to $250, usually depending on how much money can be won. Most require membership in the United States Chess Federation. In most of the world, chess sets, boards and clocks are provided, though in American tournaments, players are often required to bring their own equipment. You can find out about American tournaments by visiting the web site of Chesscity, www.chesscity.com or the USCF: www.uschess.org.

CHESS TEACHERS, COACHES, TRAINERS

You don't have to be a strong player to enjoy the international world of chess. Most tournaments are either open to all players, or have amateur sections alongside the professional competitions. Of course knowledge of the rules is essential, and no one wants to enter a competition and lose all of their games. So, in addition to chess books and software, many players turn to teachers, coaches, and trainers to get better at the game.

CHESS TEACHERS

A chess *teacher* usually works only at an elementary level. The instruction includes the rules, basic middlegame and endgame strategy, and perhaps a small opening repertoire. Chess teachers usually work in schools and at special chess camps. A good teacher will be a competitive player, usually rated at least 1700. The instruction will be balanced in all areas of the game, and the openings taught will be standard chess openings. Many teachers prefer to teach trappy openings designed to bring quick victories against inexperienced competition, but this is not in the long-term interest of the student. As many of the young masters in this book can tell you, it isn't easy to throw away openings that have become useless because opponents don't fall for the tricks. Learning a new set of openings is a lot of work, and a good teacher will build a solid foundation of reliable openings.

CHESS COACH

A chess *coach* has a different task. The coach usually works with a student only during a tournament and perhaps for a while before and after the event. There is no time to address many of a player's weaknesses. The coach prepares the student for specific openings and opponents, working within the limitations of the student's ability. The goal is to optimize results in competition, not necessarily to raise the level of the player's game significantly.

A good coach will spend some time working on endgames, because that is the hardest stage of the game to master. The coach will not try to radically change the student's opening repertoire in a short period of time, but will try to patch any holes and leaks that could lead to disaster. The coach must also offer psychological support. Young players often have difficulty rebounding from a bad game and shattered confidence. Tal Shaked, the World Junior Champion, has sometimes suffered a string of losses, and can be disconsolate even when just failing to convert an advantage to victory. Fortunately, he works with trainers who can help him overcome this. Other players become overconfident and need to be reminded of their vulnerabilities. Experienced coaches know how to handle such situations.

CHESS TRAINERS

Chess training is the most intensive and expensive form of instruction. A *trainer* provides regular lessons, and coaching and works to eliminate weaknesses and strengthen overall play. Only the most dedicated young players enter chess training programs. Trainers spend a lot of time on subtle positional concepts and endgames. They work to build a complete, solid opening repertoire and sometimes prepare special surprises for specific opponents.

Top trainers rarely impose their own opening strategies on their students. They choose from the entire range of respectable openings, picking some to fit the existing skills of the player, others to bring more experience in areas where improvement is needed. The enormous effort required to train young stars usually results in diminished performances by the trainers, whose rankings can suffer. In any case, most of the most successful trainers have been International Masters, not Grandmasters. These include Alexander Nikitin (Garry Kasparov), Bob Wade (many English stars), John Watson (Tal Shaked), and Igor Zaitsev (Anatoly Karpov), though some later went on to become Grandmasters.

Some top ranked Grandmasters have become excellent trainers while maintaining their own careers. Josif Dorfman (Etienne Bacrot), Lev Psakhis (Judit Polgar), and Jonathan Speelman (Luke McShane) are good examples. There are even examples of strong players who have almost entirely abandoned competitive play to become full-time trainers, such as Mark Dvoretsky (Artur Yusupov and many others).

Whatever your needs, choosing an appropriate instructor is not an easy task in chess, just as it is hard to select a good music teacher or tennis coach. Still, you can usually find someone in your area who can provide good chess instruction. If you just want to enjoy the game and become a better player, you can play in tournaments and take advantage of some free lessons! Play with opponents who are better than you, and make sure to do a post-mortem (post-game analysis) after every serious game.

Of course your "instructors" may not be as qualified as professional trainers, but you are likely to learn some valuable tips. Don't pay too much attention to the opening preferences your opponent might want to foist on you. Take nothing at face value, but make sure that you understand why your opponent suggests certain moves rather than the ones you played. Perhaps the opponent will be wrong, but there is usually some valuable chess logic to be learned. Naturally, if you get a chance to analyze your game with a strong player, do so! Many scholastic and even open tournaments now offer free analysis of your games by a chess instructor.

When you have played a game and don't understand why you lost, you can also try posting it to the Internet, in the newsgroup rec.games.chess.analysis. Often you'll get several interesting replies, and even Masters answer questions from time to time. Chess lessons are becoming more available on the Internet, too.

Vinay, flanked by his proud mother and coach Schiller

CHESS RATINGS & TITLES

Chess has both national and international ranking lists and titles. Any player, even a beginner, can enter the ranking list of the USCF (United States Chess Federation). To earn titles, you must perform at a required level or achieve a specified ranking. International titles require both tournament achievements and a high overall ranking.

CHESS RATINGS

Chess is one of the few sports with a completely objective ranking system. Dr. Arpad Elo worked out an elaborate formula which measures success in competition. It takes into account the level of opposition in each game, as well as the result. Points are not accumulated, because that would give a big advantage to someone who could play as many games as possible. Instead, a rating is an indication of the probability that you will win a game against a given opponent. If the players have roughly equal rankings, then the game is expected to end in a draw. If there is a big difference in rating, the higher rated player is expected to win.

The ratings range from zero to something approaching 3000, but in practice no player has broken the 2830 barrier in a published ranking. Some players have reached higher results in a single tournament.

Beginners are likely to receive a ranking under 1000 in their first competition. An average player can expect to land at 1400 to 1600. Those who work at the game and get to the 2000 mark become candidates for the title of National Master, which is awarded when the 2200 barrier is broken. At 2300 the player can seek international recognition.

CHESS TITLES

The first title most players aim for is that of Expert, or Candidate Master. That isn't really a formal title, but is the class of players rated between 2000 and 2199. The title of National Master is formally awarded when you reach 2200. Below that level, there are informal categories. These classes group together players of similar skill as players progress toward the coveted titles.

So what are your chances of reaching these exalted heights? The odds indicate that hard work will be necessary.

In addition to formal titles, we've included all the amateur classifications of the United States Chess Federation. For the American national titles, you can also see the percentage of the more than 60,000 registered players in each class.

Below is a chart that shows you the number of titleholders at the end of 1997 (rounded out to the nearest 50) and the requirements for each title.

CHESS TITLES AND TITLE HOLDERS

Title	Number	Rating Required
Class E	6750	1000
Class D	6950	1200
Class C	7950	1400
Class B	37350	1600
Class A	5250	1800
Expert (Candidate Master)	2750	2000
Master	1100 in USA	2200
	15000 worldwide	
Senior Master	250	2400
FIDE Master	2550	2300 (FIDE)*
International Master	1850	2400 (FIDE)**
Grandmaster	700	2500 (FIDE)***

*Awarded when rating achieved. Also granted to winners of World and Continental Youth Championships.

**Must perform at better than 2450 level in three major competitions. Also granted to winners of a variety of championship events.

***Must perform at better than 2650 level in three major competitions. Also granted to World Junior Champion and Women's World Champion.

FIDE refers to the International Chess Federation, which maintains their own rating list, with over 25,000 ranked players! You have to get to a rating of 2000 just to get on their list. There is also an express path. Players can earn an international title immediately by winning important championships, even junior competitions. On the other hand, only a handful of players earn those honors each year.

However, starting in 1999, FIDE will create a rating list for amateur chess (games one hour or less) that everyone can join.

There are also three titles reserved for women players. The requirements for

Woman FIDE Master are approximately 200 points lower than those for the unrestricted titles.

Take heart, however. Notice that most players fall into the class B amateur category. I started out at a lowly 869, and took many years to progress to master. Hikaru, Jordy, and Vinay all made it at age ten! As long as you are never satisfied with your rating, a little determination and study will keep your ranking moving upward, until the goal is reached.

STREET TITLES

There are also unofficial titles, casually awarded by players. A few insults, too! You will often hear the following terms used in chess conversations. A **patzer** (PAH-TSER) is a player who, in the opinion of the speaker, is not very good. Of course patzerhood is relative. To a Grandmaster, even a Master player may be a patzer. A similar term is **fish**. If you are a fish, you usually don't know enough about the game to render an intelligent opinion. A fish is always a weak player, it's not relative. If you are a **metalhead**, you are a good player, especially at fast chess. Strong 5-minute chess players often can be found on the streets of major cities, playing for money. Metalhead arose back in the days when the stakes were usually 25 or 50 cents per game. **Hustlers** are metalheads who cheat or try to win by tricks, aiming not to have fun, but simply to make money.

Usually, Grandmasters are called **GMs** (GEE-EMM) and International Masters are known as **IMs** (EYE-EMM). The title of FIDE Master is not much respected, and sometimes they are called **radio masters**, derived from the abbreviation FM.

EAT LIKE A GRANDMASTER?

When young players travel to exotic places to compete, eating can sometimes be an adventure. Some kids live off fast food, but most of our young stars adapt quickly to local cuisine. Jordy became a big fan of the rich noodle soup Siamin (known as Ramen on the mainland) while in Hawaii. Vinay usually gets home cooked meals. For the older kids, eating out is a group and social experience, as Gabe relates (on page whatever). Some players can be identified by their favorite type of candy, usually seen alongside the chessboard and scoresheet.

The quality of the food often reflects the quality of the tournament. Major commercial open tournaments are located near fast food joints, while prestigious invitational events dine at the finest restaurants. At the World Youth Championships players have been treated to sumptuous feasts, especially in Spain, where the seafood bounty is abundant. It is very easy to get spoiled!

BASICS OF CHESS

For those new to the game, chess can seem a little intimidating. There are so many pieces, and a lot of special rules! Chess is easy to learn, however, and we'll show you how to play right here. Experienced players can skip this section, which presents the most basic rules.

We will cover the chess board, the pieces and how they move, and how a chess game is started. Then we'll move on to the goals of the game, how to give check and checkmate, and when games end in a draw with no winner. Finally, we'll look at two special maneuvers: castling and en passant pawn captures. Other issues will be discussed in the Tournament Rules chapter.

THE CHESSBOARD

Chess is played on a checkered, square board, made up of sixty-four alternating White and Black squares. The smaller squares are arranged in rows of eight groups of eight, and these little squares make up several kinds of lines. The vertical lines, those running up and down the board, are called **files**, while the horizontal lines, those running back and forth, are called **ranks**. Notice that the files are lettered, from **a** through **h**, while the ranks are numbered, from **1** through **8**.

The diagonal lines, which run along a 45 degree angle and contain squares of only one color, are simply called diagonals. Note also that a light square is always in the right hand corner. It always amuses chessplayers to see how many time television and film directors get this simple setup wrong!

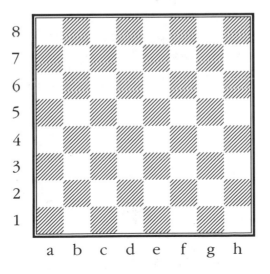

Your board may not have black and white squares. Most are brown or green and beige; some even have red squares. Chess players refer to them as light and dark, however. The same goes for the pieces. They are referred to as Black and White, regardless of the actual color. Remember to be color blind, and you won't go wrong.

PIECES

Chess is a struggle between two players who take turns making moves. Each side gets an assortment of pieces and pawns. There are only six different pieces. Each can be represented by a symbol. We use these symbols throughout the book.

♔	White King	♚	Black King
♕	White Queen	♛	Black Queen
♖	White Rook	♜	Black Rook
♗	White Bishop	♝	Black Bishop
♘	White Knight	♞	Black Knight
♙	White Pawn	♟	Black Pawn

At the start of the game, there are 32 pieces on the board, thus half of the board is filled. A correctly set up board has the White queen beginning on a light-colored square and the Black queen on a dark-colored one (queen on color), with the lower right square always being light-colored (White on right). Or think of the king as King Edward, since he starts on the e-file. The first and second ranks are set up with White pieces and pawns, the seventh and eighth with Black

The game begins when the player controlling White makes a move, and continues with Black and White alternating moves until one player traps the opposing king (this is called checkmate), or ends with one of several possible draws.

The correct setup looks like this:

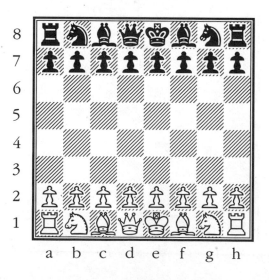

The Starting Position

GENERAL PIECE MOVEMENTS

In chess, any piece can occupy a square inhabited by an opposing piece, which is, in fact, capturing that piece. The opposing piece would get removed off the board. However, no piece may move to a square already occupied by a piece of the same color. For example, the White king cannot move to a square occupied by a White pawn or White bishop, but it can move to that square if the pawn or bishop were from the Black army, in effect taking off the enemy piece.

Let's look at each piece and learn the moves.

The King ♔

In chess, you have one **king**. The king can move one square in any direction either to occupy an empty square or to capture an opposing piece. In the diagram below, the White king can move to any of the squares with a star, and the Black king can capture the White bishop, knight, or pawn.

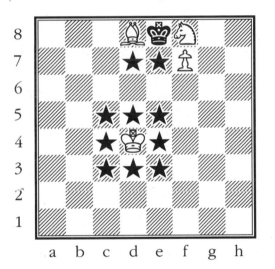

King Moves

The king can capture an enemy piece by moving to the square the piece occupies, removing that piece in the process. The king can never be captured, however. When he is threatened with capture from any enemy piece or pawn, which is called "check," the game cannot continue until the threat is removed.

The Rook ♖

The **rook** may look like a tower on a castle, but actually started out as a chariot or a ship. However, the modern rook still moves the way it always did; in straight lines, along ranks or files, any number of squares. In order to make a capture, the rook lands on the square of the enemy piece, removing and replacing it.

No jumping is allowed, so captures are possible only when the squares between the rook and the piece to be captured are vacant.

In the diagram below, the Black queen can be captured, but not the Black bishop or knight, as they are protected from capture by the piece between them and the rook.

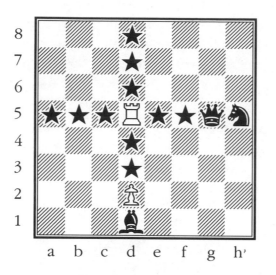

Rook Moves

The Bishop ♗

Originally an elephant in the Indian army, the **bishop** eventually took on the character of a European court rather than an army. He can move any number of squares *on the diagonal only* provided nothing is in the way. Each bishop is confined to squares of only one color; a light colored bishop will always operate on the light-colored squares, and a dark-colored bishop on the dark squares.

Bishops can capture any enemy piece or pawn on a diagonal they could normally move on, provided nothing is in the way.

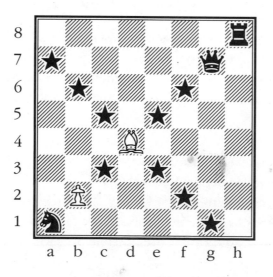

In the diagram, the White bishop can land on any square marked with a star, or capture the black queen. The Black rook and knight are protected by other pieces, and may not be taken.

The Queen ♕

The **Queen** combines the power of a rook and a bishop by being able to move any number of unobstructed squares on the diagonal, rank, or file. Besides your sacred king, which must be protected at all costs, the queen is the most valuable piece on the board as well as being the most powerful. Just move her as you would a rook or a bishop, but not both in one move. Captures are done the same way as with the other pieces.

The queen can capture the Black knight, bishop, or rook in the diagram below, but not the Black queen or pawn.

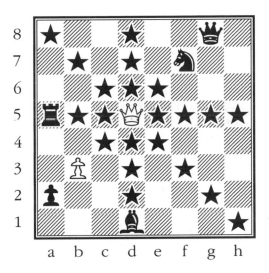

The Knight ♘

The **knight** is the only piece that doesn't move on straight lines at all, but rather, in the shape of an "L." The knight is also unique in that it is the only piece that can jump over pieces. It doesn't matter if any pieces or pawns, friendly or enemy, stand in the way. For example, the knight's first move in chess is usually to jump over its own pawns to land on the third rank as White (or 6th rank as black).

To move the knight, move two squares in one straight direction, and one square sideways. Thus, the knight cannot land on a square adjacent to where he started out and will always end up on a square of the opposite color. Look at the diagram showing all knight moves possible beginning on the d4 square to see this.

To capture with a knight, simply leap to an occupied square and remove the enemy piece or pawn that's there.

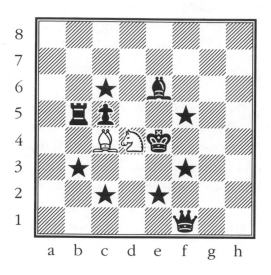

In the diagram, the knight can capture the Black bishop or rook, but not the pawn, king, or queen.

The Pawn ♙

Each side begins with eight pawns; White's side starting on the second rank, Black's on the seventh. On the very first pawn move, pawns may move forward either one square or two, provided that there are no pieces blocking that movement. Once a pawn has been moved, even if for only one square, that particular pawn may only move one square forward at a time thereafter. Other pawns which haven't been moved, still retain the option of moving one or two squares forward.

In the diagram below, we see that White and Black's e-pawns moved two squares forward on their first move, with White's second move pushing the d-pawn one square to d3.

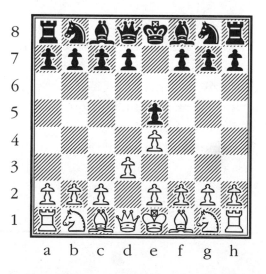

Let's say Black responds by moving his d-pawn two squares forward creating the position below. Note that Black could not move his e-pawn forward since it it blocked by White's e-pawn. If you're keeping notation, we have **1.e4 e5; 2.d3 d5.**

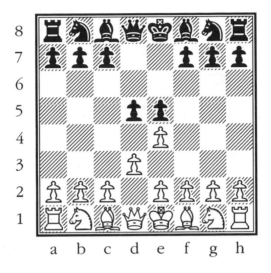

White's e-pawn is blocked from moving forward by Black's pawn on e5, however a capure is possible. While pawns may not move forward when blockaded, they may take along a diagonal one square forward! Thus, the White pawn on e4 may take Black's pawn on d5 by occupying that square. Unlike other pieces, pawns do not capture the same way they move. Pawns move *forward* but capture *diagonally*.

For other pawn moves, White could advance the d-pawn one square only, or any White pawn one or two squares. Let's say White moves **3.f4** for this position:

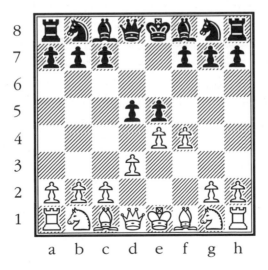

Black's e-pawn cannot move forward but it can take the pawn at f4 by moving to that square, and the d5 pawn can take the e4 pawn or advance to d4 if desired.

In the following diagram, the White c, d, and g pawns can capture, while only the Black d, e, and f pawns can capture. The White g pawn and both a pawns are blocked and cannot move at all.

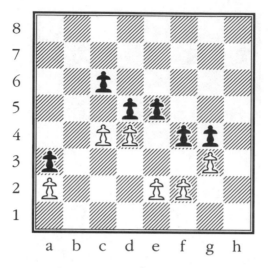

Note that pawns never move backwards. So you shouldn't advance your pawns prematurely, as you may find that you need them back home for defense! Either pawns go forward one or two squares on the first move, and one move forward thereafter, or they take diagonally, one square forward.

There are two other special pawn rules and we'll look at those now.

EN PASSANT

En passant is a French phrase meaning *in passing*. It is a special pawn move for a special situation. When a pawn moves forward two squares instead of one on his first turn, he can be captured by an enemy pawn as if he had moved forward only one square. Of course the enemy pawn must be in position to capture him if he had moved forward only one square.

As with castling, this move has extra restrictions. An en passant capture is only possible as a direct answer to the enemy pawn move. Wait a move, and you lose the right. Also, it is restricted to a pawn capturing another pawn. White can only capture en passant with a pawn that stands on the fifth rank, while Black can only make the move with a pawn on the fourth rank.

We'll take a look at an example to see how this works. Note the position of the pawns on the central files.

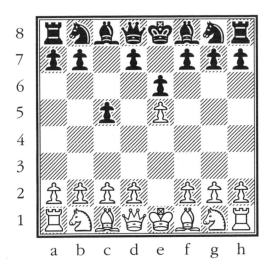

When Black advances the d pawn two squares to d6, White has the option of capturing en passant only on the very next turn. On the left diagram, the star marks the square where the capture would take place if White decides to take en passant. The right diagram shows the position halfway through the capture. The Black pawn has not yet been removed from the board.

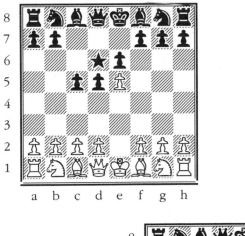

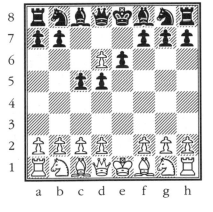

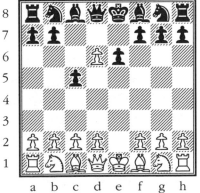

White captures the pawn on d5 as if it were on d6. The en passant capture is completed.

PROMOTION

The next exception comes when the pawn reaches the end of the file, which is the eighth rank for a White pawn or the first rank for a Black pawn. At that point, the little guy **promotes**, which means he turns into one of the pieces – either a knight, bishop, rook, or queen, at the player's choosing. He cannot promote to a king or refuse to promote. Incidentally, it doesn't matter which pieces are still on the board or which are captured. This makes it quite possible to have four, five, or even more queens on the board at the same time!

The following diagram shows both the Black pawn and White pawn one square away from promoting, the promotion squares marked by a star. Either side can promote by advancing the pawn one more square!

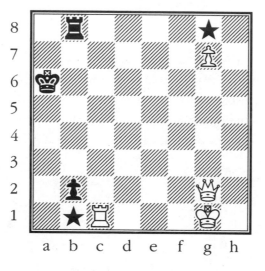

The next diagram shows an actual game featuring Irina against Carreras, World Youth, 1995. Here is the position after move 45. Let's see what happens.

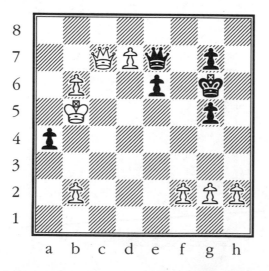

In this position Irina made a new queen by pushing her pawn from d7 to d8 at her 46th turn (**46.d8=Q**). Her opponent replied **46...Qf6**, and after the exchange of queens with **47.Qxf6+ gxf6**, Irina advanced **48.b7**. She would have obtained another new queen on her next move, but Carreras resigned the hopeless game first.

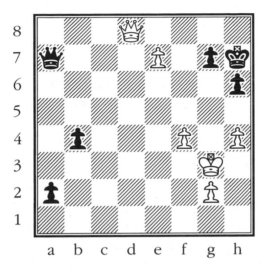

Getting a second queen does not guarantee victory, or even survival. In an earlier game, Irina playing against Bayanmonh, in the World Under-12, Girls Championship, 1994, won only because she was the first to get a second queen. Irina played **49.e8=Q** and her opponent replied **49...a1=Q**. Both sides now had two queens!

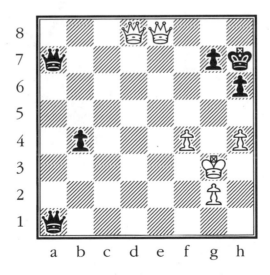

Irina now played **50.Qd3+** and Black resigned, since the only legal defense is 50...g6, and then White would deliver checkmate by capturing the pawn at g6 with the queen at d3.

To promote a pawn to a second or third queen if an extra one isn't available you to turn a captured rook upside down, or lay a piece on its side. There is always a way! In this diagram, White could promote his g pawn to a queen by playing it to the g8 square, replacing it with an upside down rook if he wants a queen. Black could promote his b pawn by moving it forward one square to b1 or capturing the rook at c1. Simply replace it with the queen that has already been captured.

CASTLING

There is a special move to help your king find safety while waking up a rook. It's called **castling**, and can be done only once a game by each player. The move has many restrictions, but first we'll get the basic idea down.

To castle, put the King next to the rook, and jump the rook over the King. There can be no pieces of either color on the squares between the king and rook.

In the diagram on the left, White is ready to castle on the kingside or **short**, while Black castles queenside or **long**. **Kingside** simply refers to the side of the board where the kings start out, while **queenside** is the other half of the board, where the queens find themselves in the beginning.

The right diagram shows the situation after castling.

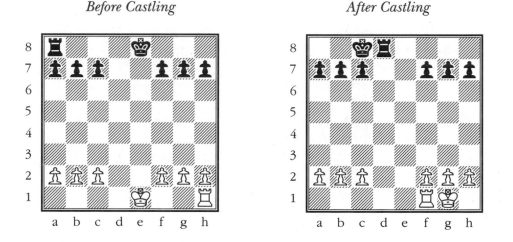

Before Castling   *After Castling*

Castling is the only time in a game of chess when two friendly pieces can be moved on the same turn. It is also the only time the rook can jump. No captures can be made during castling, and it must be the first move of the game for both the king and rook. If the king has moved, castling is not allowed. If the rook a player wants to castle with has moved, there is then no castling with that rook, though the other rook is still eligible. Also, the king can't castle into check, out of check, or through check. Since you can never move into check, it makes sense that you can't castle into check either. Let's look at the concepts of check and checkmate now.

CHECK

The king is your most valuable piece and you have to protect him at all costs. If you lose the king, you lose the game. That is why the rules require that whenever your king is attacked by an enemy piece, you must eliminate that threat immediately. When an enemy piece is in a position to capture your king, you are **in check**.

In games among beginners, the player who makes the move that places the opponent in check often says so out loud, but this is not considered appropriate in tournaments.

The object of the game in chess is not to score points or touchdowns, rather, it is to trap the king. He doesn't actually get killed or captured. When the king is under attack from an enemy piece or pawn, which means that the next move the king can be captured, it is called check. When a king is in check, everything else must be put aside until the king gets out of check. It is not possible to capture the king in chess, so the game ends if the king cannot get out of check.

> *Checkmate comes from the ancient Persian phrase Shah Manad, which means the king is helpless.*

CHECKMATE

If there are no saving moves, it is **checkmate**. Most of the time, checkmate is shortened to **mate**. (So in Australia, they sometimes say: "That's mate, mate!") When a king is threatened with capture, he *must* get out of check.

There are three ways to do this.

1. The first and usually the best way out is to capture the checking piece or pawn: The Black king is in check along the diagonal from the White queen. To get out of check in the diagram below, capture the queen with your knight.

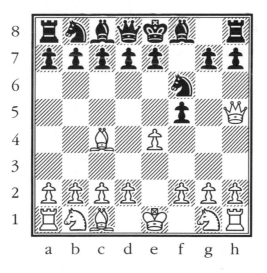

2. The second way to escape check, usually when the first way isn't available, is to block the check, which means putting one of your pieces or pawns in the way of the long range checking piece. Once again, the Black king is in check along the diagonal. This time the only way to get out of check is to block the diagonal with the g-pawn by moving it one square forward to the g6 square.

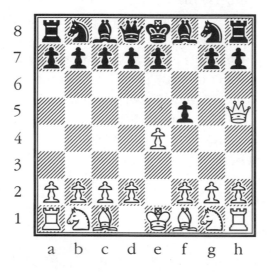

3. The third way is to move the king. Again in check along the diagonal, Black can neither capture the queen nor block the diagonal. But moving the king to the f8 square will keep the game alive by getting out of check.

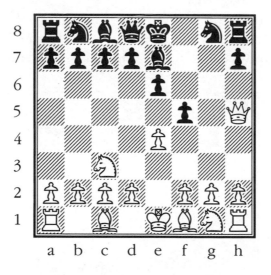

If none of these ways of escaping check are available, we have a checkmate and the game is over.

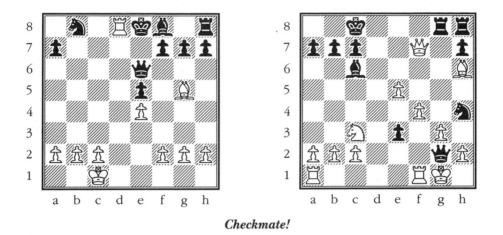

Checkmate!

MORE CHECKMATES

In order to play chess intelligently, you have to know what checkmate looks like. Consequently, here are some more checkmates. These positions are bare bones: all irrelevant pieces and pawns have been removed, including your king in many cases. All you'll see in the following diagrams are the checkmated king and the pieces and pawns required to checkmate him.

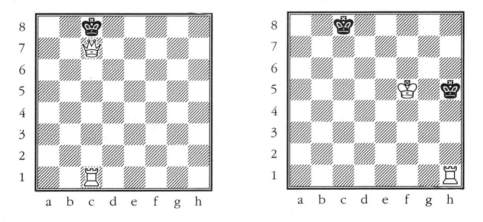

Some of these mates have funny and colorful names, while others have more descriptive names. The back rank mate can also happen on a side file. The Arabian mate comes from the early Arabian game which, like the Indian and Persian versions, used the same king, rook, and knight we still have. Legal's mate is named after De Kermur, Sire de Legal, a strong eighteenth century French player, while Anastasia's mate is named after an 1803 novel by Wilhelm Heinse, *Anastasia und das Schachspiel.*

Epaulettes are fringes worn on the shoulders of soldiers in dress uniform, and a **gueridon** is a small table. Both are French words.

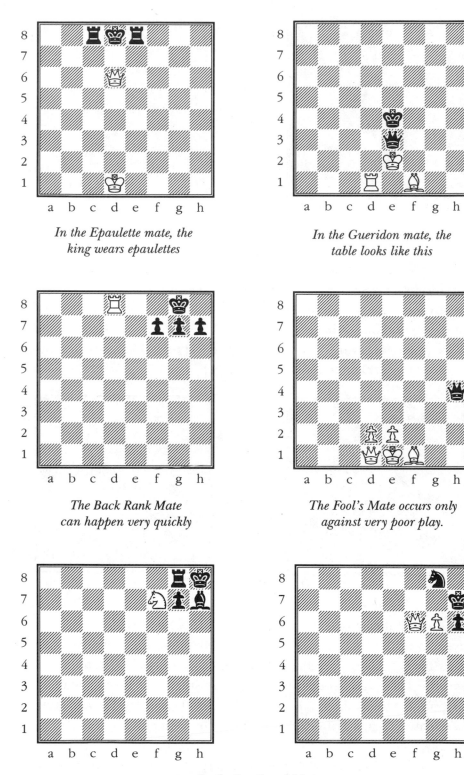

In the Epaulette mate, the
king wears epaulettes

In the Gueridon mate, the
table looks like this

The Back Rank Mate
can happen very quickly

The Fool's Mate occurs only
against very poor play.

In the Smothered Mate,
the king is smothered by his own pieces

DRAWN GAME

A draw results when neither side wins a chess game. Draws can take place by agreement or can be imposed by a variety of special rules. In the case of a draw, each player receives half a point. We'll look at the ways a game can be drawn, whether by stalemate, repetition, agreement between the players, or the 50 move rule.

In the position below, with each side having only a King, no checkmate is possible and the game will be drawn.

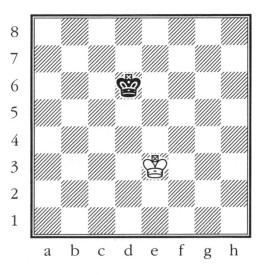

1. Stalemate

Positions occasionally occur in which the king is not in check, yet there are no legal moves. That means any possible move will put the king in check, which is not allowed. This is called **stalemate**, and the game is declared a draw, nobody winning or losing. Below, it's Black turn, but he has no legal move, thus, a stalemate.

Stalemate differs from checkmate in that the king is not in check in a stalemate while he is in check in a checkmate. A stalemate can occur with one player having most of his pieces left while the other is left with a lone king. That is the rule, however, and you should know it.

Stalemate is a factor in the artistic appeal of chess. By using the concept of stalemate, great players and composers have created wonderful artistic compositions and clever moves in actual competitions. As you will learn later, the endgames with kings and pawns crucially rely on this concept. Without stalemate, chess would be a far less interesting game.

2. Draw by Repetition

There are other ways to end a chess game in a draw or tie. Endlessly repeating the same position will result in a draw as long as one player points out that no progress is being made. Rather than make the players go on endlessly, the third time the same position is reached with the same player to move, a draw will be the result provided one of the players points this out. The rule is called **draw by threefold repetition**.

In the left diagram on the following page, the White queen follows the Black king, giving check from the d8 and a5 squares, while the poor harried monarch shuffles between b8 and a7, these squares being the only ways out of check. The alternating position is presented in the right diagram.

The extra two queens and two rooks do Black no good. A good player always keeps an eye out for perpetual check possibilities.

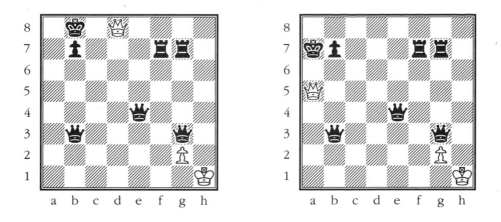

Draw by repetition, alternating checks

Matthew lost a game in the Cardoza US Open because he failed to spot this trick, even though he was offered it twice!

MATTHEW VS. TAYLOR
Cardoza US Open, 1998

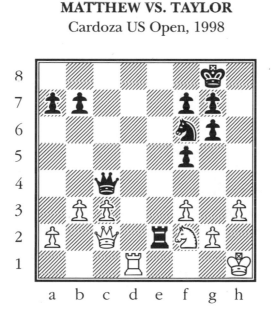

White's position is under a lot of pressure. Exchanging queens by capturing at c4 would lead to a terrible endgame, with the Black rook rampaging on the seventh rank. Matthew should have checked on the back rank, since 25.Rd8+ Kh7; 26.Qd1! Qe6; 27.Ne4! Nxe4; 28.Rh8+ Kxh8; 29.Qd8+ Kh7; 30.Qh4+ earns a miracle draw! Instead, he tried to simplify the position with **25.Rd2** and the game continued **25...Rxd2; 26.Qxd2 Qc7; 27.c4 Qe5; 28.Nd3 Qd4; 29.Qe2 f4; 30.Nf2 Nh5; 31.Qc2 Qe3.**

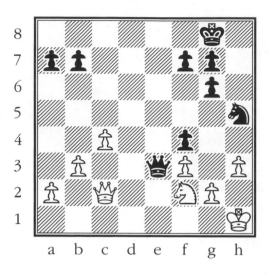

Matthew also missed a drawing possibility here. 32.Kh2 Ng3; 33.Qd1! Qxf2; 34.Qd8+ Kh7; 35.Qh4+ Kg8; 36.Qd8+ is another escape using the same trick. Instead, he played **32.Ne4** but found himself in a mating net after **32...Qe1+; 33.Kh2 Ng3; 34.Nf2 Nf1+; 35.Kh1 Ne3+; 36.Kh2 Nxc2; 37.Ng4 Qg3+; 38.Kg1 Ne3; 39.Nxe3 fxe3; 40.Kf1 Qf2#.**

3. Draw by Agreement

Another way to end the game as a draw is by mutual agreement. One player asks for a draw, and the other accepts. You are never obliged to accept a draw offer, by the way. If you think you can win, simply turn down the offer by politely saying no thank you or I'm trying to win, or just by making a move.

4. Draw by 50 Move Rule

Yet another way is available when different moves are made and the same position doesn't come up again, yet no progress is being made. If no pawns are moved and no captures are made within fifty moves, the game is declared a draw. Each of the fifty moves includes one for White and one for Black, so that's a lot of moves. This rule is meant for positions with insufficient checkmating material, which means there is no way for either player to produce a checkmate no matter how hard she tries.

King against king, king and bishop and king, and king and knight against king and knight, are a couple of examples of positions which cannot be won.

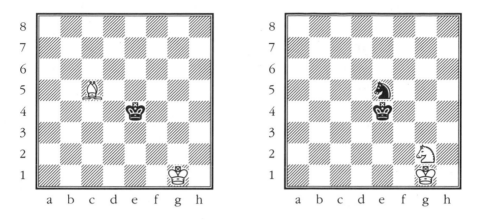

There is no way for either side to mate the other

TOURNAMENT RULES

Congratulations, you have now mastered the basic rules of the game. But we are not finished yet. In serious play there are additional rules which must be followed. Even in causal games, you should apply them so that you don't seem ignorant or rude.

The rules are not always the same. It depends on which organization is in charge. Maybe you are aware that in boxing there are many different international organizations that award titles, and each has its own rules. There are many similarities between chess and boxing, and the situation is the same when it comes to rules.

There are, at present, three international organizations which have their own rules. They are the **World Chess Federation** (**FIDE**), the **Professional Chess Association** (**WBCA**), and the **World Blitz Chess Association** (**WBCA**). International Arbiter Eric Schiller has edited this set of rules so that they apply to all organizations. If you follow these rules, you'll never need to worry about such details.

Some of the items we present are more matters of etiquette than legal rules, but we suggest that you treat them as rules, at least as they apply to your own actions. In casual games, your opponent may sometimes request that some of these rules be waived, or may not know them at all. So be flexible in friendly environments, but always behave with respect for the rules.

Touch Move

This first rule is one you should always observe, whether playing in a tournament or in class or just for fun. Always follow it, because it will build good tournament habits, which can never hurt. Losing a few games now because you refuse to cheat will make you a much better player.

Touching a piece or pawn during a chess game when it is your turn to move means that you have to move that piece or pawn. This is the **touch move** rule. Once you let go of the piece or pawn, the move is made. There is no such thing as take back. If you touch it, you move it. If you let it go, the move is made. Furthermore, if you touch your opponent's piece or pawn when it is your move, you must capture it if you can.

There is an exception to the touch move rule that you can put into operation only when you wish to adjust a piece on a square where it is perhaps off center or has fallen down. If you have no intention of moving that piece or pawn, simply say **j'adoube** or **I adjust**, which is what the French term *j'adoube* means in English. This part of the touch move rule is not, however, meant to get out of making a bad move. If you make a poor move and notice what is wrong with it while making the move or just after you made it, you cannot take it back by saying j'adoube or I adjust. Those terms are for adjusting pieces or pawns, not for taking bad moves back.

Adjusting Pieces

A good reminder is to avoid "telephone" chess (reach out and touch someone). Always check out your move in your mind before reaching out to make it. Once you get that habit, you won't fall prey to the touch move rule.

One more point about touch move is that you are not allowed to make an illegal move, such as moving into check or moving a piece incorrectly. If that should ever occur, you must move the touched piece if you can, but to a legal square. If there are no moves allowed with the piece you touched, you must make another move. There is no punishment for such a lapse.

The Chess Clock

Most chess tournaments involve many players, and the games are therefore timed. Otherwise, most players might have to wait many hours for some really slow games to end. Time limits differ, but usually give each player a set amount of time to make a set amount of moves, such as forty moves in an hour. That means each player has to complete forty moves before an hour is up on his clock. Since each player has her own clock face, that could mean two hours before each player completed forty moves.

The games are timed using a two faced clock, one face for each player. These specially made clocks, called **chess clocks**, are equipped with buttons that stop one clock and start the other when pressed. Each player has a button to press, and the way to use these clocks is to press your button after completing each move. This stops your clock and starts your opponent's clock. When the end of the time limit is reached, a little red **flag**, which begins to rise a few minutes before the hour, falls.

That means your time is up. If you have completed the right number of moves, the game goes on. If not, you lose by running out of time, just as if you had been checkmated!

In these digital times, the old timers with traditional clock mechanisms have been replaced by electronic clocks with a greater degree of precision. These **digital clocks** have also changed chess, by creating new time controls which were not available on the old **analog clocks**.

Some time limits are for the entire game, such as rapid chess, which means each player gets half an hour for the game, or blitz chess, in which each player gets five minutes for the game! These time limits are called sudden death, and make for very exciting chess indeed.

One more thing about the clock. When your game is timed using a chess clock, push the button that stops your clock and starts your opponent's clock with the same hand you move the pieces with. And be sure to remember to push that button every time you make a move! Otherwise, you could run out of time while waiting for your opponent to move, since he probably won't remind you to start his clock.

A young Jordy and Vinay hold their trophies

TWO COMMON CHESS VARIATIONS

BLITZ CHESS

Blitz chess is the most exciting form of the Royal Game. Players usually get just five minutes each to make all their moves. Whoever runs out of time first, loses, even if the position is totally winning. Pieces go flying, and tricky chess usually triumphs over deep strategic planning. With just seconds to make each move, calculation must be swift, and mistakes are common.

This speedy form of chess is especially popular with young players. Modern digital clocks allow each player to know exactly how much time is left, though many players rely on an experienced internal clock to guide their play. Hand speed is important, as many games can be decided by just a second or two. Concentration must be absolute, since any distraction can cost precious time!

The fast time control does not always mean that the better player wins. Far from it! Mistakes are common, even among the best player. Judit Polgar, ranked #16 in the world and the greatest female player of all time, won the Waikiki Blitz this summer but on the way lost a game to Jordy! We already saw that game in the Our Big Triumphs chapter.

*Irina and Gabe
go at it in Blitz !*

BUGHOUSE

One of the most bizarre forms of chess is known as "bughouse." It is played with two teams of two players each. When one team plays against another, each team gets to play with White in one game and Black in the other. When you capture an enemy piece, you hand it to your partner, who may then place it on his or her board instead of making a normal move. Gabe, like many young players, loves this strange form of chess. He and Jordy were the winning team at the Bughouse Tournament at the Cardoza US Open in Hawaii this summer.

Gabe recounts a Bughouse match...

"One of my fondest chess memories occurred in early 1997 at the US Masters in Chicago. As I recall, a number of us had very early flights the morning following the last round, and ended up staying up the whole night playing blitz and bughouse.

"The most amusing aspect of that evening had to have been Grandmaster Gabriel Schwarzman's relentless (but futile) attempts to prove himself as a bughouse player. The other players, Josh Waitzkin (of searching for Bobby Fischer fame), Greg Shahade, John Bick, Jenn Shahade and I were all experienced buggers, and were amused at the fact that such a strong chess player could be such a pathetic bughouse player.

"Game after game, Schwarzman would fall into bughouse traps tantamount to scholar's mate or fool's mate. But like any strong chess player, his will prevented him from giving up! For me, it was most satisfying in that I was not the weakest player in this game, as I often found myself in the elite youth chess circle."

ETIQUETTE

Chess players everywhere observe some rules of conduct that are traditional courtesies. We shake hands at the start of a game, and shake hands again when it is over. This is the gentlemanly or ladylike way the loser congratulates the winner, and the winner graciously accepts. It never feels good to lose, but we all do so occasionally, and it is rude to display your disappointment by crying or carrying on or any such emotional outburst. Likewise, winning might make you want to burst with joy, but don't celebrate in front of the player you just beat; it's rude.

Another common courtesy is the prohibition against kibitzing (a third party offering advice to a player during a game). Such behavior is not only impolite it is also against the rules, which state that chess is a game between two players. The time for analysis or suggestions is after the game is over. As a player there's really not much you can do about kibitzers except to ask them to stop. But you certainly can keep your nose out of other people's games when you are not playing.

In general, it is a good idea to keep quiet while chess games are going on. The royal game is not designed to be noisy. One time you can speak up during a game is to say check. Technically, announcing check is illegal in tournament chess, but common and considered polite among beginners. There is no rule that says you must, but it's still a good idea since you can't take your opponent's king if he doesn't get out of check anyway. Another time you can speak up is when offering a draw, which you will want to do when there is no possibility of a checkmate for either side.

If you are going to offer a draw during a timed game, make sure you offer it after making your move but before you push the button on your clock. And if your draw offer is turned down for any reason, don't offer again for a long time. Repeated draw offers only annoy your opponent, and it is rude besides being against the rules to do that at any time during the game.

If your opponent has offered a draw and you want to keep playing, simply say so. You can also decline the offer by making a move, but it's better manners to say something. Also, don't try to get cute by being sarcastic. One player had an easily winning position, with several extra queens and a few extra pieces, and thought his opponent should resign, so he sarcastically offered a draw. His opponent naturally accepted, and the tournament director held him to the draw.

Never ask your opponent to resign. You win by checkmating your opponent or when he gives up, not before. The best way to encourage a losing player to resign is to play the best moves. The proper way to resign, or give up, a game when you see that you're going to get checkmated, is to either say "I resign" or tip your king over. And don't forget to offer your hand.

When should you resign? Beginner's are usually advised to never resign. After all, the opponent can always make a mistake! As you get better, you find that opponents will get a bit annoyed if you play on when you have an utterly hopeless position. At more advanced levels, I think resignation is justified when you are convinced there is no way you can survive, even if your opponent plays very badly, and when all of the spectators would understand why you resigned. The last thing I want to hear when trying to get out the door after a loss is "What happened? Why did you resign?" There is no reason to resign in an endgame unless you cannot stop your opponent from obtaining an overwhelming advantage, such as a new queen. There are many tricky draws in the endgame, and the endgame is usually a player's weakest area.

Jordy's younger sister Marijo once won a game in an amazing and amusing way. With plenty of play left in the position, her opponent suddenly resigned, much to Marijo's amazement. It turns out her opponent just had to go to the bathroom, and didn't realize that it could be accomplished without giving up the game!

When the game is over, it's a good idea to ask your opponent or coach to go over the game with you, particularly if you've lost. That's the best way to find out what mistakes you have made so you can correct them in the future. This analysis is best done in another room, though. One of the most annoying things during a tournament is for nearby players to noisily analyze their game while you're still playing.

Another bit of etiquette that is very important to remember is the proper use of the word *j'adoube*. Do you remember what it means? It is definitely not meant to mean "I want to take back my move because it is bad. J'adoube is only meant for adjusting a piece or when you inadvertently brushed a piece on the way to moving something else. The touch move rule is always strictly enforced in tournaments, and it is a good idea to get into good habits from the start.

Etiquette applies to spectators as well as players. Spectators must remain silent and not interfere with the game. Normally, people watching chess games are reasonably well behaved, though a big electronic 'SILENCE' sign lights frequently during championship competition. When young players compete, it is not the uninvolved spectator that gets in the way, it is usually a parent! Chess parents are a lot like mothers of musical prodigies and young stars in dance and sports. When they get carried away, they can do some crazy things!

Here are a few examples, with names and details changed to protect the identities of people who, I hope, now realize they should have known better. At one of the World Youth Championships, the weather was unbearably hot and the playing hall was not air conditioned. One of the moms went to the tournament director's office, where the only fan on site was in use. She grabbed it, went into the playing hall, and held the fan so that it cooled her son (and only her son). The tournament officials were not amused.

Parents are usually prohibited from being in the playing area during major competitions (a good thing!), but many will do anything to be able to watch over their children's play. Sometimes they will harangue the operators of the demonstration boards (the oversized chessboards used to display games to the public) and even sometimes force their way in and take over moving the pieces on the demo board, a task for which most parents are horribly ill-suited.

Then there are the parents who are convinced their kids are the next superstars, and they steal the scoresheets, which are the property of the organizers, hoping to auction them off in a few decades for great rewards. Sometimes the theft is not for monetary reasons, but to keep the games from being published, so that future opponents will not be able to prepare effectively.

What happens when a parent and child play in the same tournament? There are many prominent father/son and father/daughter chessplayers (not many mothers in the game) who travel to tournaments together. Sunil Weeramantry, a FIDE master who is the step-father of Asuka and Nakamura, likes to play at a table as far away from his sons as possible, and tries not to be distracted by their games or let them be distracted by his own efforts. A good idea, but it often breaks down when Sunil gets into his customary massive time pressure and pieces begin flying at the end of time controls!

Most organizers would be happier if parents just dropped their kids off at the start of the tournament and pick them up at the end. This used to be normal, but the declining ages of the youngest players and a generally more protective attitude (and even laws!) has made this next to impossible. I guess I was one of the lucky young players. My parents never hung around at any chess tournaments (even those played in their own house!) and I can honestly say they never caused any grief to a tournament director. About the best a young player can do these days is develop a facial expression which lets parents know in no uncertain terms that they should not stay within sight during a game. The distractions have cost far more points than any "help" the parents can provide!

Assuming you get to play chess without too many distractions, there are a number of important concepts that will help you play better, and we'll turn to these now.

BASIC STRATEGY CONCEPTS

Now that you know how to play chess, it's time to learn to play it well. There are a few basic ideas you will have to master before you can hope to play a reasonable game, and the rest of this course will be devoted to helping you do just that. You will have to pay close attention here, for you can play quite horribly, losing game after game, if you don't apply these ideas to your games.

On the other hand, if you learn them well, you will win some games and can have lots of fun with chess for the rest of your life.

PIECE VALUES

As you recall from your lessons on how the pieces move, some pieces seem stronger than others. Beginners are taught absolute values for each piece, so that a player always knows whether an exchange of pieces is favorable or not. The truth is a bit more complicated, but when just starting out, it helps to remember the values of the pieces. These values assume that everything else on the chessboard is even, which is rarely the case.

Below is a table of their relative strength, expressed in terms of points.

Pawn:	10
Knight:	35
Bishop:	35
Rook:	50
Queen:	90
King:	1,000,000,000

The king gets that ridiculously large amount because he is priceless: if you could trade all your pieces to save your king, it would be well worth it. The rest of the pieces and the pawns are represented by their attacking power, or at least their potential attacking power.

The following is one of the most famous games of all time, and was played at the Paris Opera by Paul Morphy, one of America's greatest players, against European nobles. Let's see how he made some investments to reap big rewards.

MORPHY VS. COUNT ISOUARD AND THE DUKE OF BRUNSWICK
Opera House, Paris, 1858

1.e4 e5; 2.Nf3 d6; 3.d4 Bg4; 4.dxe5 Bxf3; 5.Qxf3 dxe5; 6.Bc4 Nf6; 7.Qb3 Qe7; 8.Nc3 c6; 9.Bg5 b5; Nbd7.

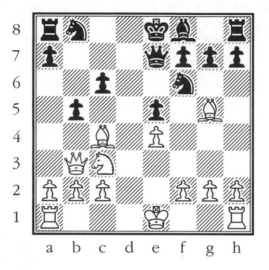

10.Nxb5 cxb5; 11.Bxb5+. Morphy traded his knight (35) for a couple of pawns (20), which left him down 15 points, worth about a pawn and a half.

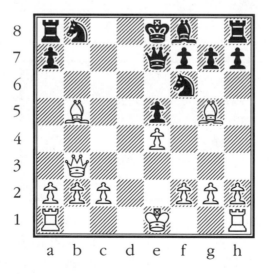

This is called a sacrifice, but it is a poor name, for his attack was worth more than 15 points. Notice how exposed the invaluable Black monarch is to the fury of the White pieces.

11...Nbd7; 12.0-0-0 Rd8; 13.Rxd7 Rxd7; 14.Rd1 Qe6; 15.Bxd7+ Nxd7.

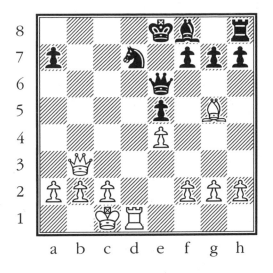

16.Qb8+ Nxb8. Morphy pays the seemingly high price of a queen (90) to further expose the enemy king, but since the payoff was the billion point checkmate, it was a bargain.

17.Rxd8#.

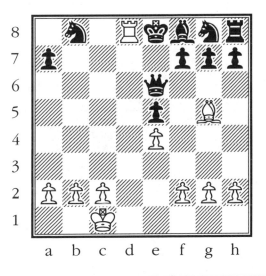

*I*t's a good idea to spend some time getting used to the differences in value of the various pieces and pawns. For instance, three pawns aren't quite worth a bishop or knight, two rooks are worth about a queen and pawn, a bishop and knight together are worth a rook and two pawns, etc.

THE EXCHANGE

One particular difference has a name of its own: a rook is worth about 15 points more than a bishop or knight. The difference is called the **exchange**. This is a confusing term, since we also talk about exchanging pieces, often of equal value. When you capture your opponent's rook and he captures your bishop or knight in retaliation, you have won the exchange, and he has lost the exchange.

CANCELING OUT METHOD

The best way to keep track of who has more points is to use the canceling out method. If you captured your opponent's knight, and she captured your bishop, you don't need to count up the 35 points for each side since they're the same. They cancel out. If you capture a rook, knight, and three pawns and your opponent captures your queen and bishop, the knight and bishop cancel out, and all you have to do is add up rook and three pawns (80) for your captures, and queen (90) for your opponent's captures. Since the difference is +10, that's all you have to remember.

Bishop and Knight cancel each other

White has 10 points more in pieces

Of course you should keep in mind that the real value of a piece depends in part on its location. A piece which is trapped in the corner of the board and which cannot take part in the action is worth less. It will take some time, perhaps even a lifetime, to develop good instincts about the relative value of pieces.

Computers try to calculate the value of position using complicated mathematical formulas, but we humans have to rely on imprecise judgement.

OVERWORKED PIECES

The value of a piece decreases as its defensive responsibilities increase. The more work a piece has to do on defense, the less it can be useful in attack. Sometimes a poor piece is given more than it can handle. Here is a good example, Vinay, vs. Yastrebov in the World Under-12 Boys Championship, Menorca Spain, 1996.

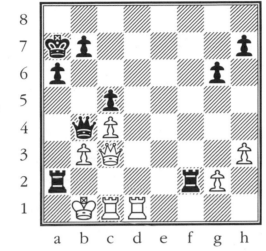

Vinay vs. Yastrebov
Black to move

White's queen must defend the pawn at b3 and the b2-square, otherwise Black moves the rook from f2 to b2 with checkmate. Vinay exploits the overworked queen by playing **35...Ra1+!!** Black resigned since the rook must be captured but 36.Kxa1 allows 36...Qa3+; 37.Kb1 Qa2#. 36.Qxa1 Qxb3+; 37.Qb2 Qxb2# is no better.

In the next example, the Black bishop is under the burden of guarding the back rank and the h-pawn. Vinay sacrifices his queen to win quickly.

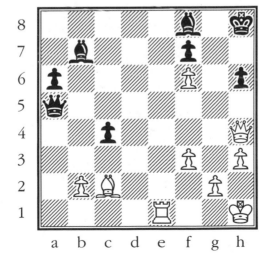

Vinay vs. Friedrich
in 1993

After **38.Qxh6+!!, Black resigned.** If 38...Bxh6, then 39.Re8+ Bf8; 40.Rxf8#.

Even a lowly pawn can be overworked, as Irina demonstrated in championship competition in Qu vs. Irina, World Girls Under-12 Championship, Brazil 1995.

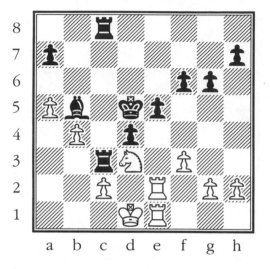

The pawn at c2 must perform two critical defensive functions. It must defend the knight at d3, but must also guard the c1-square against the enemy rook. Irina won with **43...Bxd3!; 44.cxd3 Rc1+**, and White resigned because after 45.Kd2, 45...R8c2 is checkmate.

HOW TO CHECKMATE THE ENEMY KING

To deliver checkmate to the enemy king you must control not only the square the king is on, but all those to which it may move. A king in the middle of the board is hard to checkmate because you must give check while simultaneously covering all eight escape routes.

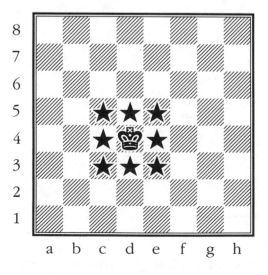

On the edge of the board, the king has fewer options.

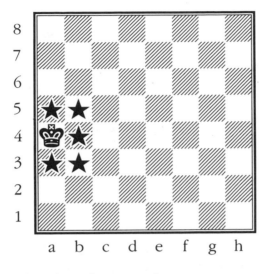

In the corner, the king has almost nowhere to run.

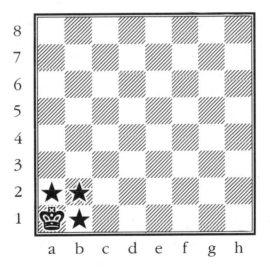

When you have to checkmate the enemy king with only your own king and a queen, you must drive the king to the edge of the board. Be careful, however, as there is a possibility that you will allow the opponent to claim stalemate if you aren't aware of an important trap.

In the following game, Matthew set up the trap, but his opponent was too sharp to fall into it.

TOM CRISPIN VS. MATTHEW
Cardoza US Open, Kona, Hawaii, 1998

If Black had played 75...Kf2?? the position would have been stalemate. Instead, Black forced the king into checkmate with **75...Qg6!; 76.Kh3 Kf2; 77.Kh4 Kf3; 78.Kh3.**

The game ended with **79...Qg3#.** There are three other checkmating moves. See if you can find them!

Checkmating with the queen is one of the most important skills to acquire quickly. Irina learned it early on, and demonstrated it in championship play. Let's see what she does.

GAUDRON VS. IRINA
World Girls Under-10 Championship, Bratislava, Czech Republic, 1993

Watch how the queen drives the enemy king to the corner. Then the king arrives to assist in the execution personally! **68...Qc5; 69.Ka6 Qb4; 70.Ka7 Qb5; 71.Ka8 Kd6; 72.Ka7 Kc7; 73.Ka8 Qa6#.**

With two rooks, checkmate is also most easily achieved at the edge of the board. Irina shows us how it is done.

IRINA VS. SERGEEVA
World Girls Under-12 Championship, Szeged, Hungary, 1994

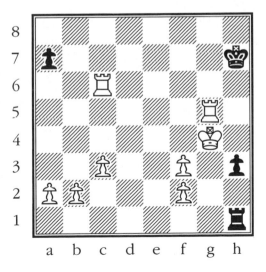

The game ended with the elegant **49.Kh5! h2.** It doesn't matter what Black plays! **50.Rh6#.**

BLUFFING

Bluffing isn't usually a good idea in chess. If your opponent finds the right reply to your bluff, your game can come crashing down. When the position is desperate enough, there may be nothing better than to try extreme measures.

JORDY VS. COSTANTINI
World Under-12 Championship, Szeged, Hungary, 1994

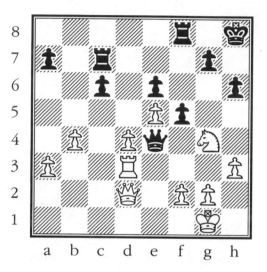

Jordy has a terrible position. The knight at g4 is under attack, and if it retreats Black's advantage of rook against knight will be decisive. Jordy tried a trick. He played **39.Nxh6.** Objectively, this is a bad move. If Black just ignores the knight, it will remain trapped. 39...Qh4, for example, would be a good reply.

Instead, Black foolishly captured with **39...gxh6??** This allowed Jordy to force mate with **40.Qxh6+ Rg7??** Black has lost his composure and the game. After 40...Kg8; 41.Rg3+ Kf7; 42.Rg7+ Ke8; 43.Qe6+ White will in any case deliver mate within 6 moves.

41.Qxf8#.

TACTICS

There are some basic tricks, called **tactics**, that can be used to gain the advantage in a game. Tactics are the little building blocks of victory, bringing concrete advantages that can add up to a winning position. The subject of tactics fills many books. Here we will just look at three of the most common ones: the pin, the fork and the discovered attack.

Pin

A piece is **pinned** when it cannot move, at least without causing great loss. If a piece is pinned to the king, it is known as an **absolute pin**. In the following position the f-pawn is pinned, because moving it would expose the Black king to check, and that would be an illegal move.

GREG VS. REEDER
Cardoza US Open, Kona, Hawaii 1998

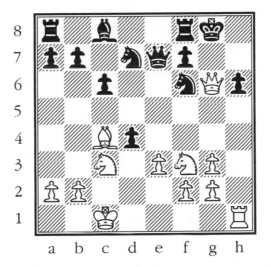

This was the position after White's; 15.Qg6+ in the game we presented as one of Greg's best, earlier in the book. The queen cannot be captured because the f-pawn is under an absolute pin. Black resigned here, not wanting to suffer the indignity of 15...Kh8; 16.Rxh6+ Nh7; 17.Rxh7#.

Fork

A fork is a simultaneous attack on two or more enemy pieces by one of your pieces. One of the most common forks is a knight attacking an enemy king or queen and enemy rook. Jordy takes on an International Master in this game.

JORDY VS. DE GUZMAN
Saitek US Masters, Honolulu, Hawaii, 1998

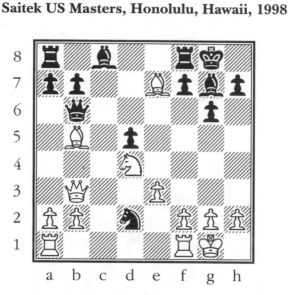

This is a classic example of the knight fork. The Black knight at d2 attacks both the queen at b3 and the rook at f1, so one of the two powerful White pieces must fall. Jordy had properly calculated that the attack on the rook at f8, and the weak pawn at d5, would provide enough compensation.

Indeed, the game was agreed drawn after **18.Qxd5 Nxf1; 19.Bxf8 Nxe3; 20.fxe3 Bxd4; 21.Qxd4 Qxd4; 22.exd4 Kxf8; 23.Rc1 Be6; 24.Rc7 Rc8.**

Jordy and Vinay ready to match wits

Discovered Attack

A discovered attack takes place when a piece moves, exposing a threat from another piece. In our example, Greg Shahade unleashes a discovered attack which is all the more powerful because the piece getting out of the way moves to a position where it can give check to the enemy king.

GREG VS. KARL SCHOFFSTOLL
Cardoza US Open, Kona, Hawaii 1998

White played **22.Nf6+**. Although this allowed Black to capture the knight with **22...gxf6**, White obtained an advantage by capturing the bishop with **23.Bxb7**. Black's weak kingside pawns were very weak, but Greg was not able to bring home the full point and the game ended in a draw.

HOW TO GET BETTER AT CHESS

The best way to improve at chess is to play, play, play! Even if you don't have a formal teacher, you can learn from your own mistakes. Actually, what you want to do is learn how to avoid repeating your mistakes. I've learned my mistakes so well that I manage to repeat many of them! The next section will point you to places where you can go and play chess, making your mistakes in relative obscurity before stepping into the tournament spotlight.

As you progress, you may find it worthwhile to join a local chess club or the United States Chess Federation. Information on chess organizations is presented in the next chapter. Of course you will make more progress if you treat yourself to some of the thousands of chess books available. To make your choice a little easier, we've included some recommended reading to get you on your way. These books, published by Cardoza, are intended for the beginner, club, and tournament level players, so you won't be overwhelmed by detail or presented with incomprehensible hieroglyphics. You should consider books from other publishers, too, but make sure that you take a look to insure that there is plenty of explanation in words, not just symbols.

If you want to take the game seriously, find a local master to teach you, or get on the Internet, where lessons are offered online. Expect to pay for the privilege, however. A good chess coach should cost as much as a good tennis coach or piano teacher. After all, they are equally accomplished professionals!

Try not to let your ambitions get in the way of your pleasure in the old game. Chess is supposed to be fun. Just as with other sports, a certain amount of effort is needed to make progress, and people have different degrees of talent. Remember that one brilliant game can earn you immortality, and strive for high quality play. Chess fans rarely remember the top finishers in a tournament, but they do recall the best games.

> *The best way to improve at chess is to play, play, play!*

WHERE TO PLAY CHESS

There are lots of ways to play chess; in person against friends or in tournaments, against your computer, or on the Internet.

CHESS ON THE INTERNET

There are many resources for playing chess and learning about the game on the Internet. The place to start is the set of Frequently Asked Questions which can be found at http://www.clark.net/pub/pribut/chess.html. The latest news is available in The Week in Chess http://www.chesscenter.com/twic/twic.html. You can ask your own questions on any of these chess newsgroups:

Rec.games.chess.misc
Rec.games.chess.politics
Rec.games.chess.analysis
Rec.games.chess.computer

A great place to start is Chess City. At http://www.chesscity.com you'll find lots of information for the amateur player, and information about the young stars featured in this book. There are also extra games, positions, and full coverage of the World Youth Championships!

CHESS CLUBS

There are chess clubs all over the country. Most towns have a place where chessplayers gather, whether it is an after-school activity, library, coffee house, or recreation center. To find a club in your area, contact the USCF or one of the state chess associations listed in the next chapter.

CHESS SOFTWARE

There are many different kinds of chess software. Some programs play chess against you, others analyze positions, and there is also software for teaching the game or improving your chess. Since new products appear all the time (and older ones disappear), we won't present a list here. You can find out about chess software on the Internet in the newsgroup, rec.games.chess.computer.

CHESS ORGANIZATIONS

There are many organizations that have control of some aspect of chess events. Some of them are global in nature, others work at a national level, and many operate on more local affairs. Most players have to pay dues to all these organizations. Usually joining the national federation, the United States Chess Federation in America, is all you need to do to be eligible to compete in rated tournaments.

WORLD CHESS FEDERATION (FIDE)

The biggest chess organization in the world is FIDE (Federation Internationale d' Echecs). It is commonly known as the World Chess Federation. Over 150 countries are now member nations of FIDE, making it the second biggest sporting federation in the world, behind FIFA, the world soccer organization. FIDE is recognized by the International Olympic Committee as the governing body for World Chess.

FIDE administers a worldwide ranking list for accomplished players and holds tournaments to designate a world champion. The World Championship was under exclusive control of FIDE from 1948 through 1993, when World Champion Garry Kasparov left the organization on a campaign to reform professional chess. So Kasparov is not the FIDE world champion, though he is certainly recognized as the strongest player in the world and has consistently topped the ranking lists, even FIDE's rating list, for over a decade. FIDE recognizes much lower-ranked Anatoly Karpov, Kasparov's predecessor as World Champion, as the World Champion, though the qualification cycle leading to his 1998 victory over Viswanathan (Vishy) Anand has been much criticized. Karpov is no longer among the top 6 players on FIDE's ranking list. Kasparov is defending his World Championship title under the auspices of the newly formed World Chess Council, facing Spain's Alexey Shirov in a match originally scheduled for fall of 1998 but now postponed indefinitely as the sponsor failed to provide the necessary millions of dollars. Efforts are being made to get everyone to agree on a single world championship format.

There is more to FIDE than just the rating list and world championship, however. FIDE organizes the Chess Olympiad every two years. Over a hundred countries usually participate. Each country can send a team of up to 6 players, and another team of up to 4 women players, to compete. In odd-numbered years, a special World Team Championship is held where only teams that survive a qualifying process can compete. There are also continental team championships for Europe, Asia, and other areas.

The World Youth Championships, where many of our young authors have competed, are held every year. Titles are awarded to the winners of boys and girls tournaments for under-20, under-18, under-16, under-14, under-12, and under-10 age groups. Many of today's Grandmasters first came to the attention of the public by winning these events.

FIDE also promotes chess in those countries that do not yet have a national federation. They constantly refine the rules of chess, and introduce new forms of the ancient game to meet the modern needs of sport and television.

Individuals do not usually have much contact with FIDE, which requires that most communication take place in official form from national federations which are members of FIDE. The official American federation is the United States Chess Federation. FIDE's website is at www.fide.com.

UNITED STATES CHESS FEDERATION (USCF)

In America, most chess tournaments are under the auspices of the United States Chess Federation (USCF). In order to play in these events, membership in the federation is required. There are special discounts for scholastic players. You can sign up online at their website: www.uschess.org. This website contains information on chess activities all over the country and is worth visiting even if you don't feel ready to join a chess organization yet. You can contact the USCF by calling (914)562-8350.

The USCF maintains a rating list for all of its members, even beginners. Our young stars all began their chess journeys with an amateur ranking. I wouldn't want to embarrass any of them by mentioning their first ratings, so I'll just mention that I entered the ranks at a lowly 867 and had to work my way up to the master level for over a decade!

For more on the rating system, see the chapter on chess ratings and titles.

STATE CHESS FEDERATIONS

You can also find out about chess in your area by contacting the USCF affiliate in your state. These organizations often have special programs for beginners and for scholastic players. Many are now on the Internet, making available a lot of useful information. You can get an up-to-date listing of state chess federations at the USCF web site, www.uschess.org.

HISTORY OF THE GAME

As with many good things, the origins of the game we now call chess are shrouded in mystery and controversy. While we know that chess was played over a thousand years ago in the Arabic, Persian, Indic, and Chinese cultures, there is no agreement where or when the game was invented. Chess is believed to have originated as a Hindu game called Chaturanga, played with four armies of kings, elephants, horses, ships, and infantry. The ship eventually became a chariot. The playing field was a 64 square chessboard. Chaturanga may have been played as early as five thousand years ago!

For a thousand years, from about 1500 years ago, what we now know as chess developed into a two player game with one army each. Each army had two of each of the pieces, but the second leader, the King, turned into a Vizier, or minister. The game had now spread to Europe and Asia.

Toward the beginning of the 16th century, ancient chess was transformed into the game we know today. The queen was introduced, as were some refinements designed to speed up the game. Now, a pawn could move two squares forward on its first move, rather than one. In addition, the maneuver called "castling" made it possible for each king to get to safety more quickly, improving the defense and making the games more interesting.

In the first part of the 19th century, chess was played primarily in cafés, often for small sums of money. Simpson's Divan, still one of London's finest establishments, was a center of chess activity in the middle of the 19th Century. Virtually all of the leading players went there to enjoy a first rate meal and convivial hospitality. Many famous and exciting games were played there.

1851 saw the first great international chess tournament, a knockout tourney held in London. Throughout the 1850's a few scattered competitions grew in importance, and by the end of the 1860's major tournaments were becoming an annual event. In the next two decades the best chessplayers would compete on both sides of the Atlantic.

As Europe regrouped after the devastation of the First World War, chess became strongly nationalistic. International team competitions commenced in Paris, in 1924. Soon there was an established tradition of chess olympiads every two years or so until the Second World War rendered it impossible. A World Chess Federation (Federation Internationale d'Echecs or FIDE) administered chess on a world-wide basis.

The Second World War took its toll on the chess world, not only losing great players, but also politicizing the game to the point where it was a feature of Cold War politics. The Soviet Union aggressively pursued world domination, and the chessboard was one of its battlefields. The tyrannical Soviet regimes held a firm grip on the chess world from 1948, when Mikhail Botvinnik brought them the World Championship, until 1972. The Soviets also dominated the team competitions, and held the Women's title as well.

Only a brash young American was able to puncture the Soviet balloon. From the mid 1950's young Bobby Fischer had been making his mark on American Chess. Temperamental and demanding, Fischer eventually managed to work his way up to challenge Boris Spassky for the title in 1972. In a match watched passionately throughout the world, Fischer fought off a terrible start but eventually prevailed, and the Soviet spell had been broken.

Or had it? In 1975, Fischer was hurled from his throne when FIDE stripped him of the title for refusing to defend it in battle. Anatoly Karpov became World Champion by default, and then defeated defector Viktor Korchnoi, whom he had also defeated in 1974, in a pair of bizarre matches that featured parapsychologists, gurus, and allegations of all sorts of shenanigans.

In 1984, Karpov faced off against prodigy Garry Kasparov, who was poised to become the youngest World Champion ever at the tender age of 21. Karpov jumped out to a 5-0 lead, but couldn't find a way to win the necessary sixth game. The match dragged out through the Moscow winter, lasting nearly six months. After 48 games, with the score now 5-3 (the 40 draws did not count), FIDE President declared the match over in one of the most controversial decisions in chess history. A rematch was ordered for September, 1985. The failure to win the match was the end of the Karpov era.

As communism ebbed, a new generation of stars came to dominate chess. Foremost among them was Garry Kasparov, who won the World Championship in 1985 and has not been toppled by any human player, though he did lose an exhibition match to the Deeper Blue computer program in 1997 after defeating Deep Blue in a previous match.

Widely considered the best chessplayer of all time, Kasparov is no less controversial than many of his predecessors. In 1993, fed up with FIDE's handling of the World Championship cycle, Kasparov held a title defense under the auspices of his own chess body, the Professional Chess Association (PCA). FIDE refused to recognize the match and scheduled their own, between Karpov and Dutch star Jan Timman. Kasparov maintained a higher ranking on the international ranking lists, and few people considered Karpov, the winner of the devalued FIDE cycle, as the best player in the world.

Chess continues to grow in stature. The 1993 PCA World Championship had a prize fund of five million dollars! Even tournaments open to everyone, not just professionals, boasted prize funds of over $100,000. Chess professionals could make a very good living, and Kasparov opened the door to lucrative commercial sponsorship from major international corporations.

- OPENINGS -

WINNING CHESS OPENINGS *by Bill Robertie* - Shows concepts and best opening moves of more than 25 essential openings from Black's and White's perspectives: King's Gambit, Center Game, Scotch Game, Giucco Piano, Vienna Game, Bishop's Opening, Ruy Lopez, French, Caro-Kann, Sicilian, Alekhine, Pirc, Modern, Queen's Gambit, Nimzo-Indian, Queen's Indian, Dutch, King's Indian, Benoni, English, Bird's, Reti's, and King's Indian Attack. Examples from 25 grandmasters and champions including Fischer and Kasparov. 144 pages, $9.95.

WORLD CHAMPION OPENINGS *by Eric Schiller* - This serious reference work covers the essential opening theory and moves of every major chess opening and variation as played by *all* the world champions. Reading as much like an encyclopedia of the must-know openings crucial to every chess player's knowledge as a powerful tool showing the insights, concepts and secrets as used by the greatest players of all time, *World Champion Openings* (WCO) covers an astounding 100 crucial openings in full conceptual detail (with 100 actual games from the champions themselves)! *A must-have book for serious chess players.* 384 pages, $18.95

STANDARD CHESS OPENINGS *by Eric Schiller* - The new definitive standard on opening chess play in the 20th century, this comprehensive guide covers every important chess opening and variation ever played and currently in vogue. In all, more than 3,000 opening strategies are presented! Differing from previous opening books which rely almost exclusively on bare notation, *SCO* features substantial discussion and analysis on each opening so that you learn and understand the concepts behind them. Includes more than 250 completely annotated games (including a game representative of each major opening) and more than 1,000 diagrams! For modern players at any level, this is the standard reference book necessary for competitive play. *A must have for serious chess players!!!* 768 pages, $24.95

UNORTHODOX CHESS OPENINGS *by Eric Schiller* - The exciting guide to all the major unorthodox openings used by chess players, contains more than 1,500 weird, contentious, controversial, unconventional, arrogant, and outright strange opening strategies. From their tricky tactical surprises to their bizarre names, these openings fly in the face of tradition. You'll meet such openings as the Orangutang, Raptor Variation, Halloween Gambit, Double Duck, Frankenstein-Dracula Variation, and even the Drunken King! These openings are a sexy and exotic way to spice up a game and a great weapon to spring on unsuspecting and often unprepared opponents. More than 750 diagrams show essential positions. 528 pages, $24.95

GAMBIT OPENING REPERTOIRE FOR WHITE *by Eric Schiller* - Players who enjoy attacking from the very first move are rewarded here with a powerful repertoire of brilliant gambits. Starting with 1.e4 or 1.d4 and using sharp weapons such as the Göring Gambit (Accepted and Declined), Halasz Gambit, Alapin Gambit, Ulysses Gambit, Short Attack and more, to put great pressure on opponents, Schiller presents a complete attacking repertoire to use against the most popular defenses, including the Sicilian, French, Scandinavian, Caro-Kann, Pirc, Alekhine, and other Open Game positions. 192 pages, $14.95.

GAMBIT OPENING REPERTOIRE FOR BLACK *by Eric Schiller* - For players that like exciting no-holds-barred chess, this versatile gambit repertoire shows Black how to take charge with aggressive attacking defenses against any orthodox White opening move; 1.e4, 1.d4 and 1.c4. Learn the Scandinavian Gambit against 1.e4, Schara Gambit and Queen's Gambit Declined variations against 1.d4, and flank and unorthodox gambits. Black learns the secrets of seizing the initiative from White's hands, usually by investing a pawn or two, to begin powerful attacks that can send White to defeat. 176 pages, $14.95.

COMPLETE DEFENSE TO QUEEN PAWN OPENINGS *by Eric Schiller* - This aggressive counterattacking repertoire covers Black opening systems against virtually every chess opening except for 1.e4 (including most flank games), based on the exciting and powerful Tarrasch Defense, an opening that helped bring championships to Kasparov and Spassky. Black learns to use the Classical Tarrasch, Symmetrical Tarrasch, Asymmetrical Tarrasch, Marshall and Tarrasch Gambits, and Tarrasch without Nc3, to achieve an early equality or even an outright advantage in the first moves. 288 pages, $16.95.

COMPLETE DEFENSE TO KING PAWN OPENINGS *by Eric Schiller* Learn a complete defensive system against 1.e4. This powerful repertoire not only limits White's ability to obtain any significant opening advantage but allows Black to adopt the flexible Caro-Kann formation, the favorite weapon of many of the greatest chess players. All White's options are explained in detail, and a plan is given for Black to combat them all. Analysis is up-to-date and backed by examples from games of top stars. Detailed index lets you follow openings from the point of a specific player or through its history. 240 pages, $16.95.

SECRETS OF THE SICILIAN DRAGON *by GM Eduard Gufeld and Eric Schiller* - The mighty Dragon Variation of the Sicilian Defense is one of the most exciting openings in chess. Everything from opening piece formation to the endgame, including clear explanations of all the key strategic and tactical ideas, is covered in full conceptual detail. Instead of memorizing a jungle of variations, you learn the really important ideas behind the opening, and how to adapt them at the chessboard. Special sections on the heroes of the Dragon show how the greatest players handle the opening. The most instructive book on the Dragon written! 208 pages, $14.95.

- MIDDLEGAME/TACTICS/WINNING CONCEPTS -

10 MOST COMMON CHESS MISTAKES and How to Fix Them *by Larry Evans* - This fascinating collection of 218 errors, oversights, and outright blunders, not only shows the price great players pay for violating basic principles, but how to avoid these mistakes in your own game. You'll be challenged to choose between two moves, the right one, or the one actually played. From neglecting development, king safety, misjudging threats, and premature attacks, to impulsiveness, snatching pawns, and basic inattention, you receive a complete course in where you can go wrong and how to fix it. 256 pages, $14.95.

WORLD CHAMPION COMBINATIONS *by Keene and Schiller* - Learn the insights, concepts, and moves of the greatest combinations ever by the best players of all time. From Morphy to Alekhine, to Fischer to Kasparov, the incredible combinations and brilliant sacrifices of the 13 World Champions are collected here in the most insightful combinations book yet. Packed with fascinating strategems, 50 annotated games, and great practical advice for your own games, this is a great companion guide to *World Champion Openings*. 264 pages, $16.95.

WINNING CHESS TACTICS *by Bill Robertie* - 14 chapters of winning tactical concepts show the complete explanations and thinking behind every tactical concept: pins, single and double forks, double attacks, skewers, discovered and double checks, multiple threats - and other crushing tactics to gain an immediate edge over opponents. Learn the power tools of tactical play to become a stronger player. Includes guide to chess notation. 128 pages, $9.95.

303 TRICKY CHESS TACTICS *Fred Wilson and Bruce Alberston* - Both a fascinating challenge and great training tool, this is a fun and entertaining compendium of two and three move tactical surprises for the advanced beginner, intermediate, and expert player. The arrangement of tactics are in order of difficulty so that a player may measure

CARDOZA CHESS LIBRARY & ORDER FORM

progress as he advances from simple to the complex positions. The examples, drawn from actual games, illustrate a wide range of chess tactics from old classics right up to the 1990's. 192 pages, $9.95.

ENCYCLOPEDIA OF CHESS WISDOM, The Essential Concepts and Strategies of Smart Chess Play by Eric Schiller - The most important concepts, strategies, tactics, wisdom, and thinking that every chessplayer must know, plus the gold nuggets of knowledge behind every attack and defense is collected together in one volume. Step-by-step, from opening, middle and endgame strategy, to psychological warfare and tournament tactics, Schiller shows the thinking behind each essential concept, and through examples, diagrams, and discussions, shows its impact on the game. 432 pages, $19.95.

- BEGINNING CHESS BOOKS -

THE BASICS OF WINNING CHESS by Jacob Cantrell - A great first book of chess, in one easy reading, beginner's learn the moves, pieces, basic rules and principles of play, standard openings, and both Algebraic and English chess notation. The basic ideas of the winning concepts and strategies of middle and end game play are also shown. Includes example games of champions. 64 pages, $4.95.

BEGINNING CHESS PLAY by Bill Robertie - Step-by-step approach uses 113 diagrams to teach novices the basic principles of chess. Covers opening, middle and end game strategies, principles of development, pawn structure, checkmates, openings and defenses, how to write and read chess notation, join a chess club, play in tournaments, use a chess clock, and get rated. Two annotated games illlustrate strategic thinking for easy learning. 144 pages, $9.95

WHIZ KIDS TEACH CHESS Eric Schiller and the Whiz Kids - Today's greatest young stars, some perhaps to be future world champions, present a fascinating look at the wrold of chess. Each tells of their successes, failures, world travels, and love of the game, show off their best moves, and admit to their most embarrassing blunders. This is more than just a fascinating look at these prodigies, Whiz Kids is also a basic primer featuring large diagrams, clear explanations, and winning ideas for young players. 144 large format pages, $14.95.

- MATES & ENDGAMES -

MASTER CHECKMATE STRATEGY by Bill Robertie - Learn the basic combinations, plus advanced, surprising and unconventional mates, the most effective pieces needed to win, and how to mate opponents with just a pawn advantage. also, how to work two rooks into an unstoppable attack; how to wield a queen advantage with deadly intent; how to coordinate pieces of differing strengths into indefensible positions of their opponents; when it's best to have a knight, and when a bishop to win. 144 pages, $9.95

303 TRICKY CHECKMATES by Fred Wilson and Bruce Alberston - Both a fascinating challenge and great training tool, this collection of two, three, and bonus four move checkmates is great for advanced beginning, intermediate and expert players. Mates are in order of difficulty, from simple to very complex. Learn the standard patterns and stratagems for cornering the king: corridor and support mates, attraction and deflection sacrifices, pins and annihilation, the quiet move, the dreaded *zugzwang*. Examples from actual games, illustrate a wide range of tactics from old classics up to the 90's. 192 pages, $12.95.

BASIC ENDGAME STRATEGY: Kings, Pawns and Minor Pieces by Bill Robertie - Learn the mating principles and combinations needed to finish off opponents. From the four basic checkmates using the King with the queen, rook, two bishops, and bishop/knight combinations, to the King/pawn, King/Knight and King/Bishop endgames, you'll learn the essentials of translating small edges into decisive checkmates. Learn the 50-move rule, and the combinations of pieces that can't force a mate against a lone King. 144 pages, $12.95.

BASIC ENDGAME STRATEGY: Rooks and Queens by Bill Robertie - The companion guide to *Basic Endgame Strategy: Kings, Pawns and Minor Pieces*, you'll learn the basic mating principles and combinations of the Queen and Rook with King, how to turn middlegame advantages into victories, by creating passed pawns, using the King as a weapon, clearing the way for rook mates, and other endgame combinations. 144 pages, $12.95.

BECOME A BETTER CHESS PLAYER!

YES! I want to be a winner! Rush me the following items: (Write in choices below):

Quantity	Your Book Order	Price

MAKE CHECKS TO:
Cardoza Publishing
132 Hastings Street
Brooklyn, NY 11235

CHARGE BY PHONE:
Toll-Free: 1-800-577-WINS
Local Phone: 718-743-5229
Fax Orders: 718-743-8284
E-Mail Orders: CardozaPub@aol.com

Subtotal	
Postage/Handling: First Item	$5 00
Additional Postage	
Total Amount Due	

SHIPPING CHARGES: For US orders, include $5.00 postage/handling 1st book ordered; for each additional book, add $1.00. For Canada/Mexico, double above amounts, quadruple (4X) for all other countries. Orders outside U.S., money order payable in U.S. dollars on U.S. bank only.

NAME _____

ADDRESS _____

CITY _____ STATE _____ ZIP _____

30 day money back guarantee!   WHIZ KIDS

Subscribe to   ssip,

Chess City is   ith the
latest news ar   nd the
world to visit   s long
before they   nings,
middlegames

Chess City is   Wide
Web. You'll b   re the
tournaments   about
the exploits o   ties of
the chess wor   rs, or
download che